Dom Helder Camara

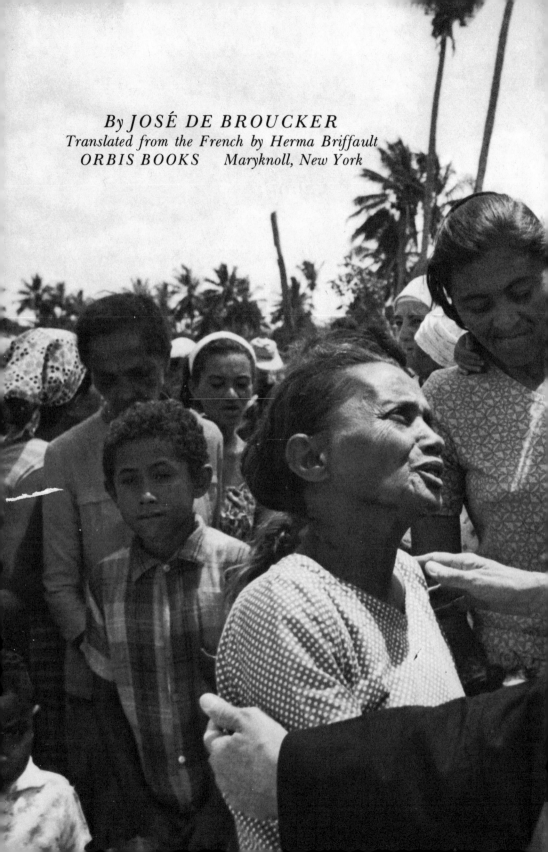

By *JOSÉ DE BROUCKER*
Translated from the French by Herma Briffault
ORBIS BOOKS   Maryknoll, New York

Dom Helder Camara
THE VIOLENCE
OF A PEACEMAKER

Second Printing

Originally published in 1969 as *Dom Helder Camara: la violence
d'un pacifique.* © 1969, Librarie Arthème Fayard, Paris

Copyright © 1970, ORBIS BOOKS, Maryknoll, N.Y. 10545
Library of Congress Catalog Card Number: 78–135536
ISBN 0-88344-0997
PHOTOGRAPHY BY JOHN PADULA, MARYKNOLL STAFF PHOTOGRAPHER

DESIGN AND PRODUCTION BY LA LIBERTÉ & RAYNER

Manufactured in the United States of America

CONTENTS

Foreword by Richard Shaull   vii

Preface   xiii

CHAPTER ONE:
Dom Helder at Home in Recife   1

CHAPTER TWO:
Victims of Injustice   25

CHAPTER THREE:
Don Quixote Rides Forth Again   53

CHAPTER FOUR:
Spokesman for the Third World   77

CHAPTER FIVE:
"I Am a Man of the Church"   99

CHAPTER SIX:
God Does Not Like Pride   123

EPILOGUE:
Dom Helder Reflects on His Life   135

FOREWORD

This book introduces a man who, though known only in limited circles in the United States, is one of the outstanding Christians of our time, a man who incarnates the anguish and hope of those who are struggling for national liberation and development in the Third World. José De Broucker has captured and interpreted, in an unusual way, the spirit, the passion and the work of this man, Dom Helder Camara, archbishop of Olinda and Recife.

This is not a time in which to exalt saints, heroes, or charismatic figures. But it is a time for encounter and interaction with those men and women who defend the cause of the "wretched of the earth" against the powers that exploit them, and who are attempting to create a new world. All of us today are in a situation in which we need to be challenged to open our eyes to the new and terrifying realities of oppression around us, to find resources for the transformation of consciousness and the development of new values, to work out concrete responses to the imperatives directed to us at this moment.

One possibility for doing this is provided when we are brought into contact with men who are living that struggle, with all the agony and suffering, hope and momentary rejoicing that go along with it. Such men call our thought and existence into question, break open new perspectives for us, encourage us to move to a new level of personal involvement, and are a sign to us that we can find life and be sustained by hope even in those situations where all the odds seem to be against us.

I know few people today who have the power to do this comparable to Dom Helder Camara. He lives and struggles in a world very different from that of most of us. His life is set in the heart of one of the most impoverished and underdeveloped areas of the world, and he is an archbishop of the Roman Catholic

Church. He has been formed by a culture with which most of us have had very little contact; his pattern of life and his spirituality may seem quite strange to us; and his ways of working for the transformation of Church and society may not be in line with ours. And yet, on the occasions I have been with him or have observed him meeting with groups of people in different parts of the world, each encounter has become an event calling forth a response not primarily to him, but to the imperatives he has brought to the center of attention. Here I will mention briefly a few aspects of such an encounter, which could also occur as you read this book.

Dom Helder is a man of faith whose eyes are fixed on the future rather than on the past. This means that he has been constantly on the move, perceiving new realities, seeking new directions, and taking concrete steps to give shape to the new. Because of this he has been forced, by the logic of his own position, to move time and again into uncharted territory, and to risk making mistakes and correcting them (as witnessed when he became involved for a time in the Fascist movement in the 1930's). Often when he has embarked on such pioneering efforts, he has drawn others into the struggle who, in turn, have moved beyond him and become a further challenge to his own position.

For some years, I have been fascinated by this interaction between Dom Helder and Catholic young people who have become involved in social and political action, in part as a consequence of his example and encouragement. Time and again such groups, being more directly involved in the social struggle, have found themselves compelled to take a more radical position than Dom Helder. Every time that this has happened, he has made a serious effort to understand them and be open to their criticism. Whenever their actions have led to their being denounced as subversive, persecuted, or imprisoned, Dom Helder has been the first to defend and support them, even though he may have been in sharp disagreement with their ideology or strategy.

Dom Helder is a man of peace, forced to live in a world of conflict and violence, take sides in it and fight. For him, the way of peace is not a mere political tactic; it is a way of life. For him, the only really human society is one in which men have learned to share the abundance of God's gifts. Anything that violates this order, even the ants eating the rosebush in his garden, perturbs him deeply. One of his great passions has been that of finding a nonviolent path to revolution in Latin America. For that reason, the life and work of Martin Luther King had a tremendous attraction for him.

Yet as he continues to follow that road Dom Helder is wise enough to comprehend that thus far all such efforts have failed in Latin America. When many of those who share his hopes and goals reject his nonviolent approach, he is deeply troubled at the same time that he understands and shares something of the moral dilemma they have faced. And like Martin Luther King, this man who does everything in his power to bring about change without violence, is himself constantly the object of vicious attacks and lives daily under the threat of assassination.

Dom Helder has taken upon himself the burden of the struggle for economic development in the Third World, and in doing so has found himself forced to work for the creation of a *socialist* society. Such a pilgrimage, on the part of a Roman Catholic bishop, cannot be brushed aside lightly. During his earlier years, Dom Helder accepted the ideologies about modernization and economic development so well known to us in this country, and gave full support to institutions and projects working at this task within the old order. Gradually, however, he came to see that the social, economic, and political structures of the old order were in themselves the major block to development, and that only as they were overcome could the problem be solved. As he put it:

> Without agrarian reform, the almost inhuman misery of the rural workers will persist. Without banking reform, little will be done for the development of the country, and without fiscal reform, the rich will continue to grow richer while the poor will continue to suffer. Without electoral reform, the elections will appear to be free but in fact will be subjected to the power of money. Without administrative reform, bureaucracy will continue to sap the strength of public life.

With this he has discovered that the whole structure of relationships between the rich nations and the poor nations is still basically of a colonial nature, and that the development of the Third World depends upon a radical change in that relationship. Thus, in recent years, he has become increasingly audacious in his espousal of socialism, and has been forced to reexamine carefully his traditional approach, as a Catholic, to Marxism and to the relation of Christians and Marxists in the revolutionary struggle. His discussion of Marxism and socialism continues to be critical, and he has encouraged the search for "new forms of socialism," but the honesty of his approach to this problem and his willingness to face and work through the hard realities of the present struggle stand out in a striking way.

Dom Helder is a churchman who would like nothing more than to devote his attention to the religious life and build up the community of faith, yet finds himself compelled to speak out on social issues and work for social change. For the sake of his witness as a Christian, he is drawn to give more and more of his time and energy to the political struggle, in his own country as well as in other parts of the world. This has meant supporting radical Catholic lay groups, sponsoring new projects of local community organizing and national programs of adult education; organizing the hierarchy for more effective action for social change; and participating in international efforts to further Third World development. As this happens, his person and his work become a center of contention in the Church and he is considered to be a dangerous and subversive element by those in power in his own country.

Dom Helder is a Christian statesman who, due to a unique combination of circumstance and personal charisma, has been offered many different kinds of opportunities to move directly into the political areas and provide leadership there. He has consistently turned them down in order to remain a churchman because he is convinced that Christian faith has an important contribution to make to the creation of a vision of social justice and to the ongoing process of personal and social transformation. Because of this conviction, the service of the Church has, for him at least, an absolute priority.

Some of us cannot accept a number of major elements in his understanding of the task of the Christian community in the social order. We are uneasy with his tendency to identify nonviolence with the Christian way, rather than to emphasize the importance of critical judgment on all forms of social struggle and on all social structures. We have little confidence in the results of his moral appeals to those in power. But his wager about the nature and importance of the Christian witness, and his willingness to pay the price of it should not only win our admiration but also raise questions about our wagers in the situations in which we find ourselves as Christians today.

Dom Helder and his closest associates belong to that small

group of men and women—at a premium in any society—who are capable of providing creative leadership in a time of transition: producing models for new economic, social, and political structures; working at difficult tasks is a disciplined way; and encouraging the best of the younger generation to participate in the work of social reconstruction and national development. Yet, faced with the urgency of this task, they find all their efforts blocked by a powerful repressive government—strongly backed by the economic and military power of the United States. Even the most moderate initiatives are often prohibited or destroyed as soon as they begin to make some impact; those best prepared to serve in different professions find that they have little or no opportunity to work at what they consider to be most important. Many of the most capable and dedicated have been imprisoned or forced into exile; a few have been killed.

Here Dom Helder is living daily with one of the most excruciating problems of our time: What are the grounds for hope for those who are powerless and know only one defeat after another? How does history move forward in the face of such opposition and in the midst of so many casualties? What is the meaning of participation in a long-term struggle in which many will know only frustration and failure? There are no clear rational answers to these questions today that make much sense to us, but there are a few people around the world who keep going—and help keep others going—hoping against hope. Dom Helder is one of these. He combines, in a unique way, intense suffering and a spirit of joyous abandon.

Dom Helder is a man of the Church, who believes in the institution and in its reformability. He has seen the need for radical reform at many points, and has used his extraordinary gifts as a strategist to work for such change. His hard work over the years to build up the National Conference of Brazilian Bishops and his pressures on the Church to recover its lost poverty are only two examples of the many initiatives he has taken in this regard. What is more unusual is the fact that he gives even greater attention to all sorts of experiments which might provide some clues as to the shape of the Church of the future. His decision to have seminary students move out of an impressive new building before it was even completed, live in small communities in the slums, and structure their program of theological studies around the problems of national development as experienced in that situation—this is one symbol of Dom Helder's freedom to move ahead in daring new ventures for the sake of the Church of the future.

Some of us would raise questions about his trust in the institutional Church and his hope for movements of renewal or reform. We would also make other wagers about where we expect new forms of the Church to emerge and how we work toward that goal. But we share his emphasis upon the importance of "Abrahamic minorities" in the Church and we may find it important to work at the task of giving structure to the life and witness of such groups in dialogue with Dom Helder as well as with others of more radical persuasion.

After having mentioned all these things, I confess that what most distinguishes Dom Helder is a certain quality of saintliness. It is reflected in his whole being and irradiates to those around him. His extraordinary openness to and concern for people, especially the very poor; his willingness to bear the suffering of men and women, and of the world, within himself; his espousal of poverty and simplicity of life; his charity toward all, even those who attack him most viciously; his constant struggle with pride; his patience, humility, and enjoyment of simple things; his celebration of each new day as a holiday; and above all, his freedom to move with the Spirit of the Lord at any moment into the unknown: all these are marks of a modern saint.

Most of us don't know what to make of saints. Their presence tends to remind us of a world we believe long since past. But they also call our attention to the fact that in this age of transition, we too must develop disciplines which make for constant transformation of consciousness and of life. As we go about that task, we may learn a great deal from those whose existence has been shaped by a rich tradition, even as we find it necessary to express the reality witnessed to by that tradition in radically different ways.

RICHARD SHAULL

Princeton Theological Seminary

PREFACE

Who is Dom Helder? The question is still sometimes asked, amazingly enough. For it could be expected that everyone, by now, must have heard of this bishop of the *favelas*, those terrible slums of Rio de Janeiro, this tireless marcher in nonviolent demonstrations, this thorn-in-the-flesh of the "reactionaries."

Many people know him, or think they know him, but in fact few really do. Only a few intimates know how much more complex and multiple and surprising and rich are his life, his work, his soul, than they appear to be on the surface.

I myself had read his works and had read a great deal about him, had even met and talked with him many times. But when I visited him in his small house at Recife and began collecting material for this book, I realized that I knew very little, indeed almost nothing about his life before the year 1964 when, as archbishop of Olinda and Recife, his speeches, travels, and actions brought him to the forefront not only of Church history but also the history of underdeveloped countries and of the world.

Thus it gives me pleasure to share with others what I was privileged to hear from Dom Helder himself.

JOSÉ DE BROUCKER

Levallois-Perret

Dom Helder at Home in Recife

If it depended on me
I would suppress
all iron bars,
all hedges,
all walls.

If it depended on me
doors and windows—
except for the rare moments
when they must shield
the King's secrets—
would remain open,
generously letting in
the air and light and life!

PERNAMBUCO, OCTOBER 26-27, 1968

1

Dom Helder talks about himself pleasantly and simply. Not complacently; there is no fatuity in him, he has the true simplicity of a child. But how call childlike the manner of a man so prudent, who weighs his silences, measures his words, controls his gestures, calculates his risks, and foresees his effects? A child, this politician who gives presidents wakeful nights, who overturns two generals in less than three years, and whom the Oppositions quarrel over in their search for someone to embrace their causes? A child, this champion of civil rights who can sway crowds with his words? A child, this prelate who has been received by the pope eighteen times and was one of the centers of interest at the Vatican Council, the man who manages to unite in his person the prophet and the churchman? A child, this manager who can set up an operation and make it succeed, who knows how to capture the necessary money wherever it is and how to administer it?

Then, can it be that his simplicity, his cordiality, his readiness to serve, and his poverty are merely cleverness and politics, the consummate artistry and subtlety of an expert in public relations, and of a born comedian to boot?

I am aware that these are the questions asked about Dom Helder, among a few others. I have the feeling that Dom Helder asks them of himself, in the sensitive depths of a lucid and demanding conscience. But mainly I want to assert that I have proved that they all fade away in his presence, as we talk with him and listen to him talk. The few hours and days I have spent with Dom Helder count among the rarest moments of human and spiritual truth that can be granted anyone to live.

How can I share this rare experience with others?

I was doubtful of the possibility of doing so when the French publisher, Fayard, suggested that the method should be a series of interviews or "dialogues" if, that is, Dom Helder would agree to it. The following letter was his first response:

> "My dear friend, José De Broucker
> "To say yes to your request is to accept the idea of the 'Dialogues' that Fayard asks you to write. To say no is to take a position that you do not deserve.
> "It is for you to decide whether you will come or not. Here in Recife you have and always will have a brother in Christ."

Obviously he did not at all like the idea of this book. Later on I became even more convinced of this. That he agreed to it was obviously merely out of kindness. I have never known Dom Helder to say no to a request that was not manifestly mean; I have seen him hesitate, make an almost imperceptible gesture of annoyance and distaste, have detected a glint of impatience in his eyes. But then immediately, as if regretting these reactions, Dom Helder almost invariably decides to capitulate. He may not see the good that can result, but in any case he does not want to reject what might be some unknown plan of Providence. Rather than trust his own prudence, his natural tendency is to have confidence in the other person, which is a way of having confidence in life. I have never seen him turn away a photographer or journalist. Yet he could find plenty of excuses or even good reasons to do so.

*   *   *

As I left the Recife airport, alone, carrying my bags, looking for a taxi, I felt sure the archbishop was out of town, otherwise he would have been there to welcome me as I stepped down from the plane. He would be incapable of doing otherwise, for I knew his custom of welcoming a visitor: it was not to wait for his arrival at the house but to put all else aside and go to the terminal.

I had been told that Dom Helder had moved out of the "Episcopal Palace" a few months earlier, but I still did not know his address, having merely been told that it was a small, inconspicuous house in one of the parishes of the town. The cab-driver did not know the address, either, so he took me to the Episcopal Palace.

Dom Helder invariably speaks of that palace with a kind of sad and ashamed irony: "The so-called Episcopal Palace," he will say, or "What they call the Episcopal Palace"—and so on.

More than a year before his arrival in Recife, in January 1963, Dom Helder told his fellow members of the Vatican Council how eager he was to see the Church go boldly "in search of her lost poverty."[1]

He spoke these words just after the first session of the Council, when he was auxiliary archbishop of Rio de Janeiro and was living in a small room of his sister's home.

"We must not allow our house to be called a palace, and we must take care that it really is not one." And he continued:

"There is a theory that can be historically proved: before undertaking reforms in depth, the Church has always had to come to terms with poverty. Let us take the initiative and suppress our personal titles of Eminence, Beatitude, Excellency. Let us lose the mania of considering ourselves nobles and let us renounce our coats of arms and heraldic devices. Let us simplify our attire. Let us not have our moral force and authority depend upon the make of our car. Let us pay serious attention to our place of residence.

"Important as all this is, it concerns our outer aspect, one might say. The essential thing is our mentality. Let us have the courage to examine our conscience and our life. Have we or have we not adopted a capitalistic mentality, do we or do we not employ methods and proceedings quite suitable to bankers but not very suitable to a representative of Christ?

"Providence has already delivered us from the Papal States. When will the hour of God come which will bring the Church back to rejoin Lady Poverty?"

That hour would not be long in coming for the new archbishop of Recife, but he was obliged to live in the Episcopal Palace for four years. His contained wrath can be felt in the apostrophes he was to utter in Rome, at the end of the Council in December 1965:

"We, the *Excellentissimi*, need a most excellent reform. We have had enough of a Church that wants to be served and demands to be always the first served; a Church that lacks the humility and realism to accept the condition of religious pluralism; a Church that proclaims *opportune importune* (2 Tim. 4:2) that she has a monopoly on truth. Enough of prince-bishops who keep themselves at a distance from the people and even from the clergy!"[2]

Still, today at each cross street in Recife are signs that direct the cab-driver: "To the Episcopal Palace." Dom Helder would naturally prefer them to be replaced with others that would direct people, for example, to the House of the People, or, quite simply, to *Manguinhos*.

Manguinhos is the name of the palace. It is a large mansion with impressive flights of steps and colonnades surrounded by a space that looks more like a shabby and dusty playground than a garden. It stands on Ruy Barbosa Street and, for Dom Helder, who is fond of symbols, that is enough to express its purpose, since Ruy Barbosa was one of the most prestigious fighters for the emancipation of the African slaves in Brazil, toward the end of the nineteenth century.

My not being expected at the palace was enough to indicate that Dom Helder no longer resided there. A bedroom was put at my disposal, however, and for the duration of my stay in Recife this was to be my home. The big house was airy, with all doors and windows opened wide. As they always are, I learned, not only to let in the breeze from the sea, which is not far distant, but to let out the suffocating tropical heat, and also to show that the house belongs to the people and is open to them.

Next day I was to see the crowds that constantly fill the big tile-floored reception room, crowds of the anonymous poor, augmented from time to time by delegations of priests, students, peasants, sometimes journalists in a hurry, all of them waiting to speak with the bishop.

He receives in the adjacent room, the door being left open so that anyone approaching it can see the long table covered with a green baize cloth, at the end of which sits a dumpy little man, his clasped hands resting on some closed file folders; this is the archbishop of Olinda and Recife, and he is listening intently to one of his visitors. He seems quite unhurried.

With its sideboards and its pictures of the Last Supper, this room was no doubt the usual dining room of the archbishops who resided here in the past. Today it looks more like a corridor. From everywhere, through the always open doors, can be heard the sound of voices, telephones, typewriters. One hears singing, discussions, for there are people at work here, although no one seems to be working very hard. Dom Helder's assistants come and go, handing him a paper or folder, asking for information or advice, or decision, or a signature. At set hours thermos bottles of hot, sweetened coffee or glasses of orangeade and plates of cookies are carried into all the nooks and corners of this beehive.

In the evening, at the sudden fall of darkness, the shutters close and Manguinhos empties. At night, I was to be the only inhabitant of this house and a single light would continue to shine there, the one facing the stairway on the first floor. It lights the only room that resembles Dom Helder slightly: the chapel, admirable in its quiet plainness. On the wall above the tabernacle is a great wooden crucifix.

"That was the gift of a man who lives in a shanty," Dom Helder explained to me. "But after he carved that crucifix he made a dozen of them. They sell very well, because it is now fashionable to have a crucifix carved in wood."

Dom Helder is often the last person to leave what is still called the Episcopal Palace. Unassumingly he walks away, a worn black briefcase in his hand, not sorry to leave.

How, and why, did he live there for four years, up to March 12, 1968? No doubt because he did not think he should follow his own desires without any concern for others.

He had often, so he told me, thought of opening the garden and the palace to accommodate at least some of the many ill-housed people who exist in the muddy environs of Recife. But the palace is not his property; it was handed over to him by his predecessor and he must, in his turn, hand it over to a successor. The house belongs to the diocese, therefore it is up to the diocese to dispose of it, and perhaps the diocese is not yet ready to do what Dom Helder could wish. Man of the Church, as we shall see, Dom Helder never likes to act independently of the Church.

That fact exists and has its penalties. He has a particularly painful recollection of the two episcopal thrones he found in the palace upon his arrival. He managed to get rid of one of them rather quickly; the second one took longer. If I understood correctly, that throne was in the big reception room where most of the meetings take place. One day all the seats were filled except the throne, and some men were standing as they waited. Dom Helder overcame with difficulty the reverent fear of a poor peasant who finally agreed to sit on the episcopal throne.

"That day," Dom Helder said with a smile, "I comprehended Christ the King."

He retains an almost unendurable memory of the crowds of poor people who waited at the doors of this vast mansion, jealously shut upon its emptiness. One image remains in his mind like a nightmare.

"All those people who peered at me through the windows

when I was eating my meals! Like patient oxen. It spoiled my appetite."

At last, on March 12, 1968, the archbishop was able to leave the palace. He comes there no longer except in the daytime to be with and work with the others.

Since, by force of circumstances, Dom Helder had been unable to meet me at the airport, it gave me great pleasure to go to meet and welcome him upon his return. But I was not alone. Dom José Lamartine Soares, his auxiliary bishop, an episcopal vicar, and a few friends and collaborators were already there, waiting for his arrival on the plane from Rio. Night had fallen, and a light breeze fluttered the coconut palms.

"Dom Helder will be tired, don't you imagine?" I asked.

"No. That puny little man defies fatigue."

Only five feet three in height, weighing only 118 pounds, over 60, with the appetite of a bird and incessantly active, it is a wonder how Dom Helder keeps going, but he does. And I have seen him fatigued, in the early morning, before saying Mass, when his face has not yet recovered its liveliness, or again in the evening when his voice ceases to "speak" and he only talks in a slightly dull and muffled tone. But this never lasts long. Apparently he cannot bear to be seen or to feel fatigued; he makes an imperceptible effort to be "present" to another, and again life floods him, flashes from his eyes, his lips, all the dramatic mobility of his countenance, his arms, wrists, fingers, hands always trying with unimaginable energy to make everything bear witness—you, the table, the heavens.

Dom Helder scarcely sleeps, and no doubt it is in what he calls his "night watch" that the secret of his vitality and stability must be sought.

"Ever since I was a seminarian," he tells me, "I have had the habit of rising at two o'clock in the morning. I set my alarm clock, and I am then very fatigued. But it is at that moment that I achieve an inner unity. During the day I am pulled apart in all directions: one arm stretched here, the other in another direction, this leg, then the other. We must recover our inner unity, especially our oneness in Christ."

Two o'clock in the morning is when Dom Helder reads his breviary, prays, and writes his little meditations in the form of poems. It is the time when, no doubt, he recalls all those stories of another world, peopled with all God's creatures, from the angels to the ants, stories he sometimes unguardedly recounts to his friends, half apologetically.

"For me," he says, "transition from the natural to the supernatural, from reality to dream is almost imperceptible."

It is also the hour when he works, prepares the mail that he will give next day to his secretary, replies to certain letters, writes his conferences—in French or in English sometimes—regulates the countless affairs in which he has a word to say, and sometimes has the first or last word. Church affairs: regarding the archdiocese and the suffragan sees, which make up the ecclesiastical province, the pastoral zone, which includes the dioceses of the Northeast, the realm of social action of the Brazilian episcopacy, and the Latin American bishops' council. And then, there are his concerns with the affairs of men: the Bank of Providence; Operation Hope; the movement Action, Justice, and Peace; problems of the peasants, the workers, the students, the army, and businessmen.

The "night watch" begins at two o'clock in the morning and lasts a long time, to judge by all the affairs that occupy his mind.

Yet just as ritually, Dom Helder makes himself go back to bed and sleep again before saying early Mass. And if his parish does not require his presence elsewhere, he says Mass at six o'clock or a quarter past. One wonders how he manages to keep going.

"You see," he explains, "I have the great good fortune to be able to sleep whenever I want to and no matter where. When I trust the driver, I can easily fall asleep in a car. And also in a plane."

A woman friend has told me she once saw him sleep quite tranquilly as he sat upright in a chair in a sacristy, while waiting for the bride and groom he was to bless. He was all ready, wearing the alb. As it happened, the fiancé did not put in an appearance: his family had objected to the marriage and had sent him far away. The archbishop had only to declare the ceremony annulled. He had not completely wasted his time.

"Occasionally, too, I would very much like to sleep, but people want me to talk. It was like that today. After three fatiguing days of conferences, meetings, discussions that lasted until late in the evening, I had looked forward to sleeping in the plane. But a lady who got in at Rio came to sit down beside me, and listening to her problems took up all the time until we arrived at Recife."

Dom Helder steps down from the plane. He reaches the barriers behind which people wait for the travellers. I wonder if I shall be able to speak to him. Five, ten, twenty persons recognize and approach him, exchange an *abração*, a few words, sometimes more than a few. And at the center of a cluster of human beings the diminutive figure of the bishop disappears as he goes slowly toward the great glassed-in waiting room.

There the cameramen's spotlights flash. Is it television or cinema? I do not know. Anyway, some journalists, pen and notebooks in hand, are there. Dom Helder yields to them, agrees to pose, answers questions—and does all this with a smile that expresses patience more than pleasure. The baggage room is only a very short distance away, but it takes another five minutes for him to reach it, so hemmed in is he by all the people who are there to welcome him. Giving twenty pats on twenty shoulders, Dom Helder says how-do-you-do twenty times, says twenty goodbyes, sends twenty messages of friendship that actually show a personal interest.

I have seen the same thing on other occasions. I recall Dom Helder at Orly, when he passed through Paris in April 1968, for a brief halt, coming from Rome on his way to Strasbourg. A few of us had formed a group to converse with him in a small room provided for this purpose. An airline hostess had been entrusted with the duty of seeing to it that everything went smoothly and that the Brazilian visitor should not miss his plane to Strasbourg. I believe this hostess remained anonymous to the rest of us, to us she was merely a discreet and efficient silhouette. But not to Dom Helder. I recall how he took special pains to thank her.

One memory brings another. A few days later, Dom Helder was again in Paris. Before he delivered his address, some members of a society to which I belong were gathered round a dinner table. That evening, his special attention centered on the young woman at whose home the dinner was given.

"My dear lady, you haven't eaten anything!" he remarked at one point. "Really, you must eat something."

He had noticed, he had paid attention.

*　　*　　*

Dom Helder does not own a car. That evening we rode in the small "Auto-Union" car of the young president of the Theological Institute. I must say I cannot visualize him at the steering wheel of a car, and can even less imagine him employing a chauffeur. And, I will add, he really does not need a car.

"Of what use would it be?" he says, when I make these remarks. "I go into the street, I walk toward the place where I want to go, and before I have taken twenty steps a car draws up to the curb and someone calls out, 'Hello, Dom Helder. Where are you going? Let me take you!' And so, I get into the car and am driven to my destination. It is always like that."

And indeed that is the way things are. Whether in broad daylight or pitch darkness, whether Dom Helder is seen full face or profile, whether advancing or retreating, everyone recognizes this little man with his round beret flattened down on a head with a bald spot on each side. His well-cut black garbardine coat, which does not entirely conceal the cassock that has no trace of violet, helps identify him, and so does his unhurried way of walking, with occasional halts. Dom Helder does not talk while walking; he walks while talking. His footsteps and his halts punctuate the rhythm, the twists and turns of the conversation.

And a car stops for him. The driver may be a man or woman, a cab-driver or a bourgeois or a businessman, the car may be a Volkswagen (so commonly seen in Recife) or a North American car, the kind favored by the "upper class." And Dom Helder does not have to be urged; for him, this is a privileged occasion to meet and know people, an occasion he cannot let pass. He questions, he listens, he leans toward the driver. He learns how people live, learns about their families, their problems. And that night he will remember all this when he prepares his conference for the next day. Some people read newspapers to find out about the world; he prefers to find out about the world by travelling in other people's cars.

However, on the drive from the airport to his house, Dom Helder did not listen. Instead, he talked, twisting around on the front seat to make himself better heard by those in the back, above the night wind that came through the open car windows. He told about his trip to Belo Horizonte, where he had lectured. And had met "Such remarkable young people!" He had sponsored a new class in engineering and had found the students "remarkable"—he repeated the word. He had attended a dinner given by the staff of the great newspaper *A Folha de São Paulo*. They had just purchased another newspaper, it was now an enormous chain. "And the editor-in-chief, having heard my address, told me I could count on his group to work for Action, Justice, and Peace even if it cost him a lot! That's tremendous!"

There had been, in Rio de Janeiro, the annual Festival of Song, and Dom Helder had missed none of it, for he believes that song is an important thing to every Brazilian of the Northeast, and believes that today still, as it was a hundred years ago, the breath of liberation and revolution comes through the theater and song.

"The jury awarded first prize," he said, "to the classic lyric, *Sabia*, named for our commonest bird. But when the audience of young people stood and gave a tremendous ovation, it was for the second prize, a magnificent song of protest."

From this subject, Dom Helder went on to discuss a recent merger about to be concluded in France, that of the Fiat and Citroën companies, and he was as well informed on this point as any constant reader of *Le Monde*. It was one more item, a big one, in the demonstration he was trying to make to the big and small capitalists of Brazil and the Third World, who refused to see that their so-called "free enterprise" was in fact nothing but a toy in the hands of the great international trusts.

Dom Helder had been invited to accept the title of honorary citizen of São Paulo; this was an award not to be missed, for in that capital of Brazilian capitalism he was called "the Red Archbishop of Recife." São Paulo represented a challenge that Dom Helder could meet.

The picture Dom Helder was painting was clouded by one care: Cardinal Agnelo Rossi, archbishop of São Paulo, had just agreed to accept an official decoration from the hands of the chief of state, Marshal Costa e Silva, on the president's birthday, which happened to be the anniversary of the launching in Brazil of the great nonviolent movement, Action, Justice, and Peace. An active portion of the clergy and laity was scandalized, felt that the cardinal should have refused the decoration and instead should demand the return of Father Pierre Wauthiers, the French worker-priest who had recently been expelled from the country for having taken part in a justified strike. Those priests and those laymen wanted to "break off" with the cardinal, and this worried Dom Helder who, with the aid of a Protestant pastor, had tried to settle the disagreement by peaceful means.

"There must be no violent action!" he exclaimed. "What we need is dialogue. Especially now that the cardinal has reversed the measures he had taken against the professors of philosophy and theology. In doing so, he has proved that he is a man who can engage in dialogue. We must help and encourage him. What we need is dialogue!"

In this affair, Dom Helder was rather optimistic and his optimism was justified for, three days later, all the newspapers were in an uproar over the refusal, *in extremis*, by Cardinal Rossi, to accept the honor the president had wanted to bestow upon him. On the other hand, he was less optimistic about another affair that was shaping up quite far away, in Baltimore, Maryland.

Two priests, three former missionaries, a Christian Brother, and three laymen were about to incur heavy penalties there for having demonstrated against the Vietnam war by spectacularly destroying some draft files.

"They have sent me an appeal, saying, 'Dom Helder, it is for you and for the Third World that we acted. Come to witness in our defence.' What shall I do? I must go there, of course! But I cannot go without first seeing the American bishops and learning whether or not my intervention will create problems for them. I have telegraphed my friend Bishop Wright of Pittsburgh asking him to reply, by wire, saying whether I should go to Baltimore or not. I'm still waiting for that telegram."

He waited every day for it, and it did not come, at least not while I was in Recife, which I left when the Baltimore trial was only two days distant. I could see that he was very preoccupied.

How long did that drive last, from the airport into town? Thirty minutes, forty minutes? At any rate, time enough to measure the universe without secrets or limits in which Dom Helder moves. It also lasted the time required to reach his house, which now has nothing of a palace about it.

*   *   *

The house in in Rua Enrique Diaz, a street named in memory of the black leader of the guerilla war against the Dutch in the seventeenth century. At the corner is the church of the *Fronteiras*.

"In Portuguese," says Dom Helder, "the word means frontiers, boundaries, and also barricades. Come into my house."

Taking a key out of his pocket, he opened a green-painted wooden gate, and introduced me into his garden. Could it be called a garden, that space of about ten by twelve feet between the high white walls of the house, the church, the street, and a neighbor's house? Yes, and better and more than a garden: a whole world.

"Look at my rosebush. It's still small but is growing, and one day it will climb up the wall and go over it right into the street."

As he spoke, his hand swept a wide arc, evoking that future color and perfume. He went on to tell something of the rosebush's story.

"One morning, as I was leaving, I saw that the ants had eaten the leaves of my rosebush. That was serious! I bent down, picked up an ant, and holding it in my hand I looked it directly in the eyes and talked severely to it: 'Why are you eating my rosebush? I insist: why are you eating my rosebush?' Then the ant gave me a lesson. Trembling all over, it looked at me and replied: 'Why should you be the only one who has the right to enjoy the rosebush?' Yes, that was a lesson!"

The story had a sequel, but Dom Helder did not tell it until later on, when we were at table.

"I'm the one that shows up badly in this affair. I said to the ant, 'Why didn't you eat all this grass, here, instead of my rosebush?' And the ant did not reply. But next day when I went through the garden I noticed that the grass was not looking at me. And I said to myself, 'Tch, tch, Dom Helder! What did you say?' "

Again, continuing the subject, Dom Helder said, "Why cannot the rosebush, the ants, the grass, and mankind share life with each other instead of warring to the death? It poses problems. God the Father, in his goodness, had to base life on death. We call certain animals hyenas because they eat carrion, that is to say, corpses. But we are doing the same, aren't we? Meat, fish? We merely clothe them in agreeable colors. Life always supposes death on every level. For me to be here in Recife, another archbishop had to die. It is a mystery. Life, life only without death, life springing from life and not from death—that exists only in the Holy Trinity. But afterward, when God wants to make something and scatter his riches about a little, he must be satisfied to create incomplete, unfinished, weak creatures. It is a great mystery."

But this latter conversation occurred on another day. That evening of his arrival, Dom Helder showed me over his house: three rooms and a bathroom.

With rapid step he crossed the first room to open the window and the shutters, giving a view of some tall coconut trees: it is the garden of the nursing school kept by nuns, the Daughters of Saint Vincent de Paul. All day long through the window comes, along with the air and sunshine and birdsong, the tinkling of the convent bells, the singing and laughter of young girls.

In front of the window is stretched a big Amazonian hammock; this, and a small round table covered with a cloth, three chairs, and a lamp hanging from the ceiling, swayed by the wind, comprise the entire furnishings of that room. On the white walls there is nothing but an image of the Virgin of Guadalupe fashioned of reeds. It is here, in the morning or evening, that one may see Dom Helder and talk tranquilly with him. But many people have found this out and know that they can knock at the street door any time of the day or night. Dom Helder has a keen sense of hearing and will open the door.

The adjacent room is the study. It contains an armchair, a big table stacked with papers that leave only a small surface free for writing, books on the shelves, a typewriter, a phonograph and records. Late in the evening, early in the morning, it is here that Dom Helder prays and "achieves inner unity," reads, writes, and studies. Behind a screen is a small table on which the nuns deposit a thermos of hot tea for his "night watch."

On the middle of the worktable a photograph occupies a prominent place.

"Oh!" I exclaimed. "That is Father Michel."

It is the portrait of Cardinal Suenens, archbishop of Malines-Brussels. And it evokes the "complicities" of the Vatican Council. When the cardinal, sitting at the table of the moderators, pushed his spectacles up on his forehead, his friends knew that he had a problem to solve and that ten minutes later everyone would have an opportunity to discuss it. And when the cardinal wished to communicate with certain bishops, he did so by telephoning into town. On the telephone he introduced himself by saying, "Father Michel here . . . " Dom Helder has entertained for him great esteem, friendship, and affection.

On the shelves, within reach, I noticed an album of photographs of Father Louis-Joseph Lebret, founder of the movement "Economy and Humanism" and IRFED (Institut International de Recherche et de Formation en vue du Développement Harmonisé), the father, or you might say the uncle of the encyclical on the Development of Peoples—of all mankind, of man. Beneath entirely different aspects, there was much in common between the Breton of France and this Northeast Brazilian: the same contained but obstinate passion for justice.

Impossible to call to mind all the personages of today and yesterday who people Dom Helder's universe. However, there is one I will go out of my way to mention. His effigy is in the study, a naive statuette in ceramic. It is Father Cicero. I had often heard Padre Cicero talked about as an extraordinary person who draws crowds to him in Northeast Brazil and from farther off. I had come to confuse his image with the one that, at a distance, I had composed of Dom Helder, so I was not surprised to find him here in this house. Later on, when Dom Helder presented him to me, I realized that there are as many differences as affinities between these two men, between these two natives of Ceará, both equally popular and equally priests, but as different as men as they are different as men of God.

Another detail attracted my attention: in the exact middle of the worktable reigns a small porcelain statuette of a doe. The little animal carries a basket on its back which the nuns fill with fresh flowers every day. To tell the truth, I did not notice it until after I went into the adjacent room, a high-ceilinged and narrow room with a narrow skylight. The low divan, with its neatly drawn coverlet, looks minuscule there. And on a low table stand a dozen small porcelain does! And on a chest of drawers, surrounding a small statuette of Saint Francis, are another dozen porcelain does! On October 4, after saying Mass, Dom Helder had assembled all of them for a fete in honor of the *Poverello's* birthday.

"Dom Helder, why this predilection for does?" I asked.

"We call them *corças* here, or *corcinhas*. *Bicho*, corresponding to your French word for them, *biche*, is the name we give to all the charming little animals. And *bichinhas*, 'little beast,' is a pet word, a very sweet cajolery. In Brazil, lovers always call each other *bichino, bichinha*. But when we speak of the female deer, we say *corça*, or *corcinha*.

"You see, one day I was travelling by car through a forest, I believe it was between Geneva and Fribourg. Suddenly we saw a notice: *Attention, cerfs!* Beware! Deer! My interest was aroused and at the same time I was a little afraid. Then, all of a sudden, there on the road was an animal of the deer family, but instead of a stag or deer, it was a doe. I opened the car door and got out. The animal came toward me, very slowly, and she directly entered—"

He paused, opened his arms wide:

"—my heart! Then she went away. Since then, whenever I tell this story, my friends give or send me these little porcelain does. Now you know!"

But one cannot follow Dom Helder very far on that forest road which imperceptibly leads from reality to dream. Is it true, as some say, that he was given a live doe which he entrusted to friends nearby and that he goes to visit the animal from time to time?

*　　*　　*

This house of the archbishop of Recife is not, properly speaking, a house. He wanted to take the neighboring house, which was for rent, but the rent was too high—the equivalent of about $42 per month. That house would have looked poorer, because it is a little old house typical of the region, crouching low, with its door and two windows opening directly upon the street. But it would have been less poor.

And so Dom Helder chose the less spectacular but more economical and honest negotiation and had what had been the sacristy of the *Fronteiras* church remodeled for his living quarters. His bedroom is separated from the baroque high altar only by a wooden partition, and as he wakes he can hear the nuns' Mass being sung at about half past five. His study communicates directly with the present sacristy. He need take only a few steps to be at the altar facing the people. But at six o'clock in the morning there are almost no people. There may be perhaps a few nuns prolonging their thanksgiving prayer, a few passersby who drop in for a moment before doing their shopping at the nearby market, the Mercado Derby. But this does not matter. For the Mass and for prayer, Dom Helder seems to have no need of a crowd, of a congregation. The Mass, which he says slowly, without affectations, very "classically," more like a hermit than a country priest, is Dom Helder smiling upon the new day.

And the day's work begins immediately afterward. Only rarely does anyone come to his Mass without the idea of being able to talk tranquilly with him later, and one goes quite naturally from the sacristy to his house. There the nuns have left everything needed for a breakfast that Dom Helder will barely taste, but not without enjoyment.

After breakfast he will go out, shut and lock the garden gate, walk a few yards, then get into a car that a friendly soul has drawn up to the curb, and go down to the Episcopal Palace where he will work with his secretary. At noon, he will leave the Episcopal Palace, walk a few yards, get into another proffered car and go down to the school kept by the Belgian Sisters.

"I have my lunch there—a matter of fifteen minutes and it's

over," he tells me. "Because I have laid down my conditions. At first they prepared a big room for me. One of the Sisters went back and forth a dozen times to serve me. I said, no, no, I didn't want such a thing. I demanded that they find a small room for me, close to the kitchen, and that a casserole be set on the table holding my entire meal, at one go."

The casserole is a pretty baking dish with compartments for the meat or fish, the rice, or the potatoes. Fifteen minutes: that is a short time for lunch, but enough time for him to have still more visits. For example, that big husky priest, Father Paulo Santos. Dom Helder explains that case to me.

"He is a priest of a diocese in my province, in a region where the oppressors of the poor are terrible. Two months ago his life was threatened and he had to abandon his parish and come here. Now his bishop wants him to return. And he too wants to return. Today, at three o'clock in our Manguinhos, he will meet with his bishop, a representative of the stockbreeders Father Santos defends, the secretary for agriculture, and the head of the military establishment of the governor of Pernambuco, with the object of studying ways to put pressure on the big landowners."

The way will be found.

In the afternoon, Dom Helder goes to Manguinhos to see people and to work with his collaborators, as we have already seen.

"And what about the evening meal? Do you dine at 'Drive-in Derby'?"

"Well, yes, often. Or else at someone's home. But I believe my little secret has been laid bare. The Sisters suddenly were afraid that I would do without dinner, so they too have bought a compartmented casserole and have told me they will leave my meal on the table every evening."

I recall at least three evenings spent at Recife in the company of Dom Helder.

That first evening, he had dined on the plane. But being very solicitous about me, he took me out to a nearby restaurant along with other priests who had also met him at the airport. We went out about half past eight, after I had been shown over the house, and although we had to walk only a short distance there were delays, so that I believe we did not sit down to table much before ten o'clock.

On our way to the restaurant we met a young man who was

particularly anxious to talk with Dom Helder. He wanted to ask him to come at once to preside over a closing session of the third week of a course in odontological prophylaxy at the college close by. A brief consultation ensued, Dom Helder wondering how and why he could refuse. Everyone agreed that he should accept the invitation, we all thought it would mean a delay of no more than five minutes, so we all went.

The lecture hall was filled to bursting with students of both sexes. On the platform were chairs and a table covered with foliage and flowers. Applause greeted Dom Helder's entrance and the meeting resumed, with a few speeches and the handing out of diplomas. Warm applause was given to Dom Helder when he spoke a few words. I noticed that a few young people here and there did not applaud.

"The most radical ones are no longer with him," someone whispered to me.

I thought we would leave at once, but some group photos had to be taken with the archbishop in the center. The five minutes stretched out to three quarters of an hour. But this delay gave me the opportunity to see Dom Helder "in his element"— enjoying himself with a crowd of young people. Fatigue, the passage of time no longer counted for him. And I recall certain key words of one of his speeches: "Let us open, while there is still time, a bold and unlimited dialogue with youth, in full confidence, for the young do not accept a half-confidence. After all, and I address you, my adult listeners: the young are your offspring, are they not? You think they go too far? It is normal that there should be exaggeration here and there. When the day comes that our young people are moderate, prudent, and cold, like old people, then the country will die of disgust."[3] And again, "Woe betide the parents who try to suppress the impetuosity of the young and who, for lack of intelligence do not profit by the criticisms made by these implacable but loyal judges; and woe betide those who, for lack of heart, do not benefit by the warmth of those who are conscious of their responsibility in the construction of the world!"[4]

At the restaurant Dom Helder is known and treated as a neighbor. The proprietor was Italian, his wife was French. And that Italian *patrón* is surely the only person I ever saw trying to kiss the ringless hand of the bishop. They were very happy to serve him and hoped that Dom Helder would agree soon to bless their new house.

"*Muito abrigado*—thank you very much," said Dom Helder. It was he who was grateful. Why and how could he refuse the request?

Between the *pizza* and the pear tart, I mentioned the wind of pessimism blowing over the Catholic intellectuals of Europe as a result of the repeated blocking by the Holy See of a number of openings made by the Vatican Council. Above all, I was thinking of the pope's journey to Bogotá, of his appeal to the generosity of the rich and powerful, of his condemnation of violence, which he said was "neither evangelical nor Christian." Many had been disappointed, some were scandalized among those who, on both sides of the Atlantic, are engaged in the struggle for the emancipation of the poor.

Not so, Dom Helder. Or rather, it seemed to me that he refused to see things in such a light.

"Why stop at what stops instead of coming to an agreement with what is agreed? In Paul VI's address at Bogotá there are a number of admirable things that permit us to go ahead. For instance, he has not condemned those who believe they should resort to violence; he has even recognized that they might have very noble motives for doing so. If you examine his pronouncements as a whole, you will not find a single phrase, a single address you can object to. As I always say, before Bogotá, there was the encyclical on the Development of Peoples, and that allows us to go far!"

There is no way to make Dom Helder speak ill of anybody, especially the pope. Everything is "for a good end." Ecclesiastical prudence, is it? Or spiritual wisdom? Or invincible optimism? He has great confidence in Paul VI. He is pleased to think that the letter to the peoples of the Third World,[5] which grants the right to the poor of poor nations as to the poor of rich nations to defend themselves against "the subversive war of money," and which he signed at the head of the signatures of eighteen bishops in July 1967, was not in the least frowned upon by Rome. And yet he has the moral certainty that this document did not escape the attention of the pope. He trusts the clear mind of Paul VI; for example, he knows why the pope put aside the idea of a journey to Czechoslovakia, foreseeing many months in advance the events of August 1968. He trusts the attention Paul VI pays to public opinion, his constant effort to maintain the prestige and authority of the Holy See.

"The pontifical scales will soon dip on the other side" is one pronouncement of Dom Helder that I have noted.

We were strolling calmly back toward Enrique Diaz Street when a powerful North American car suddenly drew up to the curb beside us. It was eleven o'clock at night. The driver was a journalist on the staff of a big North American news agency. An appointment was made for the following morning.

On another evening Dom Helder wanted to take me to dine at the "Drive-in Derby" restaurant on the beautiful tree-planted Derby Plaza. There, as the name indicates, meals will be served you in your car. We settled down on the terrace under a loud-speaker blaring out music not of the best, although Brazilian.

A car drew up, a man got out and approached Dom Helder. After the usual greetings there was an exchange of a few words and the man drove away.

"He is a man of the *sertão*," Dom Helder explained. "He recognized me and merely wanted to say hello."

"How can so many people know you?" I asked. "You do not wear the purple ribbon or the pastoral ring of a bishop. And your pectoral cross is, to say the least, unobtrusive."

"It's television. Up to two months ago, I had a very simple television program. I've lost it now. The management, those who had entrusted the program to me, finally realized that my talks were unsuitable. Of course you are aware that I am a 'subversive'?"

Some students passed by, paused, turned back. After shaking hands with us and exchanging some news, they left us.

"I enjoy sitting here," said Dom Helder. "Right next door there is a student center, and the students come out by that front door. I am fond of the students. Sitting here, I see people."

Dom Helder ordered for himself a ham and cheese sandwich and Coca Cola; for me he ordered chicken à la Brazil. Some urchins not more than five or six years old hovered round us, begging. Dom Helder drew them to his side, one by one. He did not give them money, but told them to order a sandwich and he would pay for it.

"You walk these streets as if you were universally loved," I said, "yet you know that is not the case. You have been threatened, quite definitely."

"I often receive anonymous letters, but I destroy them without reading them."

"In May 1968," I continued, "we heard of an attempt on your life that might have succeeded if the killer had had a few less scruples."

"Yes, poor fellow! He told me everything. 'I'm a personal friend of So-and-So,' he said, 'and he rendered me great services in the past. He told me to come to Recife and ask you for help. He said you would do nothing for me, just as you do nothing for anyone because you are an egotist. And he said when you refused to help me that would be the moment to strike. But I told him I was your friend and that you have often helped me. But he insisted, declaring you would do nothing for me and then I was to use force against you!'

"But that poor fellow did not understand what the other meant by 'use force.' He asked Mr. So-and-So to explain and was told, 'That priest must be eliminated.' And the poor fellow told me, 'You don't have to believe me. I am talking like this to you because I feel sure you won't do anything against Mr. So-and-So. But I warn you! Another poor man like myself may do what I haven't the courage to do.'

"Now, I ask you, how could I assume the right to beware of a poor man if I see Christ in him? No, the whole thing is incredible."

"Haven't you ever considered," I asked, "that you should take some special precautions?"

"To begin with," said Dom Helder composedly, "I believe there is no real danger, for the moment. Two years from now there may be. It will depend on how effective our movement is. I refer to the movement we call Action, Justice, and Peace. And then I recall President Kennedy, and his brother Robert, how they were surrounded with bodyguards."

"You are not afraid of death?"

"No, and it's this absence of fear that should perhaps disturb me, since I know, as a priest, that the ones who die most tranquilly are those who have most feared death during their lifetime. But old age, you know, brings a rather poetic image of death. I remember how Christopher Columbus behaved when in mid ocean his sailors mutinied against him—and how joyful he was at the first sight of land. Thus, old age gives us something like the hope of an imminent landing!"

Again, on our way back to his house, Dom Helder was stopped by someone: a sociologist, a laicized Jesuit.

"A remarkable man!" said Dom Helder as he saw this person approaching. And he explained to him that the telegram he was expecting from the Pittsburgh bishop had still not come and that he could not be a witness at the Baltimore trial without it and without being quite sure that his testimony would be justified. End of the colloquy.

But the day's work was not yet over. Inside his house, Dom Helder removed his Roman collar and loosened his cassock at the throat, then put a coughdrop in his mouth. No sooner had he done this than there was a knocking at the door. It was a Brazilian newspaper reporter who had come for certain documents. Then, another knock at the door. This time it was a woman and her daughter. Dom Helder invited them to come in and sit down.

The third evening that I recall happened to be the last night I spent in Recife. It was half past eight. I had come to Dom Helder's house to pick him up. He was writing statements for the next great public demonstration of the Action, Justice, and Peace movement. He immediately put down his pen.

"Dear friend, good evening! I must tell you about the sin I committed today. I neglected to buy the phonograph record—"

He had promised to buy a certain record for me, having noted from one of our conversations that I particularly wanted to take a record home with me as a souvenir of my travels. He had noted it, then forgotten.

I gave him a little plastic *sabia* I had bought for three farthings from a peddler in the town. He was unfamiliar with this trinket. You put water in it and then blow, to procure a twittering as of birds. He went into the bathroom to fill it and try it out; he came back very pleased.

"This will provide some fun tomorrow. Did you hear? The cats replied to the twittering!"

That night we went to the theater: the first-night performance of a quite young theatrical company to which Dom Helder had granted the use of an outbuilding of the Episcopal Palace. The play was *Le Malade imaginaire*. Dom Helder seemed to know everyone in the audience. He took a seat without bothering about protocol—a protocol that does not in fact exist there. At the theater he felt at home. He recalled for me an evening when, in Rio, he had gone to see Jean-Louis Barrault's production of Claudel's play *Christophe Colomb*. He was in a cheerful and confidential mood. And in the course of this conversation I learned, but without being able to note it down, about the "moral pressure" he was bringing to bear on his council to get rid of the second episcopal throne in the Palace and how he dispenses with the crosier, his auxiliary bishop's crosier sufficing quite well in case of need, and how his assistant priest has a hard time on ceremonial days, picking up his miter, which falls off every time he bends down to greet the children.

Molière is for all time and all places, and his *Malade imaginaire* well survives the voyage to the tropics and a Brazilian adaptation. The show was over just before midnight. My plane left at two o'clock in the morning. Dom Helder absolutely insisted on accompanying me to the airport. As if by chance, a friend happened to be driving there. The plane was one hour late. Dom Helder would not leave me until I had gone through the exit door of the airport toward my plane, at three o'clock in the morning.

That three-hour wait at the airport was the shortest such wait I ever spent in my life. Not a trace of fatigue showed in the eyes or the voice of Dom Helder. Our conversation was of no importance, we talked about everything and nothing, that is to say, all those nothings that are the essence of humanity and in the long run of Christianity, the world where, beneath the big systems and conflicts and statistics, men live and die, suffer, seek, struggle, all those weak men we must help. We talked as if we expected to be with each other next day.

When we parted, I wondered if I had begun to comprehend the simple and radiant consistency of this elusive bishop, who has a certain way of seeing and living all creation, of seeing with the heart more than with the eyes, of seeing with the inexhaustible hope brought by faith.

N O T E S

1. "An Exchange of Ideas with Our Brother Bishops," Rome, January 1963, unpublished.

2. "A Postconciliar Period Worthy of Vatican II," press conference in Rome, December 1, 1965.

3. Guest lecture at the School of Philosophy and the School of Social Service of the regional University of the Northeast, at Campina Grande, December 11, 1966. Cf. *Revolução dentro da Paz*, Rio: Sabia.

4. Address at the Institute for Research on Brazilian Reality, Brasilia, June 21, 1967, unpublished.

5. "Message de quelques évèques du Tiers-Monde," *Témoignage crétien*, August 31, 1967.

Victims of Injustice

Ended thy miracles,
finished thy triumphs!
Get out,
disappear
without meeting the multitudes
as quick to hiss as to applaud!

I pity the masses
that require portents
but shun the every-day
and exult at the unexpected, the unusual,
who are childlike, infantile,
and whom the demagogues
nourish with sweets,
encourage with gestures,
amuse with chimeras.

RIO DE JANEIRO, OCTOBER 2, 1950

2

The plane that brought me from Salvador and from Rio closely follows the coastline. Far below, one sees a narrow band of white foam stretching out in a narrow ribbon; long ago, apparently, the continent and the ocean signed a treaty dividing up space. From one point to another there are greenish lagoons and brown rivers that seek without much conviction to join the open sea. Narrow ochre roads traverse the well-kept zones of verdure, and encircle the elevations that are worn down, crushed, bald, carved with quarries having sharp edges, as if a rain of meteorites had pelted the region. In the sunlight and seen from above, this country does not at all give the desolate impression that one imagines upon hearing the phrase "a quadrangle of hunger." Nonetheless, it comprises the entrance to that quadrangle.

We describe a wide circle at low altitude before setting down on the landing strip. I look for the town of Recife. Only four years ago I had passed this way and I believe I have a good memory. But when I look for familiar landmarks, I find none. I see the Recife of my memories everywhere, but as if the town had multiplied; to the right, to the left, bordering the sea, beyond the airport, in the interior, on all sides the horizon is now outlined with great buildings.

At ground-level I have the same impression as the taxi takes me toward the Episcopal Palace. The long straight road no longer seems to be what it was, a desert road running toward an oasis. Today it is an avenue lined with machine shops and factories, buildings well lined up and set back slightly from the pavement. There is work here; the many trucks on the highway prove it.

As we reach the city, the trucks give way to Volkswagens, a herd of them in bright colors, sparkling chrome, either taxis or private cars. This, also, is not a part of the memory I had kept of

Recife. I do not recall such movement, such activity, such a quantity of money.

With such obvious prosperity, why is Dom Helder perpetually protesting? This question occurs to me and during my entire stay in Recife, this time, I shall find myself asking it, in some form or other, very often. The country, the town, are so visibly benefitting from an accelerated development! Then why not say so? Why perpetuate the image of direst misery? Here, as anyone can see, a wealth of imagination, energy, and dollars has been invested by government and individuals, by capitalists and technicians to create the conditions of a modern economy. Why risk discouraging these well-meaning people by continuing to talk of negligence, exploitation, and injustice? Suddenly, at the very center of this anthill of more than a million inhabitants, I find myself wondering if Dom Helder, whom I have heard decry time and time again the established disorder, may not be mistaken, may not be misinforming the world!

Naturally I have seen the misery that co-exists in Recife: an entire little world of cripples and ragamuffins holding out their hands to the passersby and waiting an eternity in the street. But after one has seen the slums in Caracas, Bogotá, Lima, Quito, Asunción and even Rio de Janeiro, one finds the famous capital of the Northeast showing up to advantage by comparison, and undeserving of the incomparably bad reputation it has been given. Yes, of course, I have been shown the *mocambos*, the *favelas*, the *alagados*, the *invasoes*, and various other shantytowns; but, precisely, they had to be shown to me, because they do not spring to view so overpoweringly and outrageously as do the slums of so many other cities in South America. And even, of the infamous slums rotting in the pestilential swamps in the southern portion of this town, what I mainly recall, after having seen them, is the fact that they are gradually shrinking in size.

Then, if things are really as I see them, how understand and explain the unflagging combat waged by Dom Helder? How avoid seeing in it, as so many ironical and furious adversaries see in it, at best, a futile prophetic fuming in reverse, detached from reality, and at the worst, a kind of demagogy deliberately subversive?

Such were the questions I asked myself as my taxi entered Recife. They were gradually answered, as I listened to Dom Helder. To begin with, the problem is not merely to see things as they appear to be, but to know how to look at them. I had to look through the archbishop's eyes in order to see beyond what my tourist's eyes saw, and to understand something other than what the distinguished economists had explained to me.

"To understand the Northeast, one must understand development *per se*, and to understand development in Brazil one must understand the Northeast."[1]

We may add to that statement by Dom Helder, that in order to understand both development and the Northeast, one must at least know something of SUDENE—the Superintendency of the Development of the Northeast. Ever since 1959 this organization has taken charge of stimulating and planning the efforts aiming at the development of this portion of Brazil.

At first, when Dom Helder was still in Rio as secretary-general of the Brazilian bishops' conference, and for a while afterward when he arrived in Recife as archbishop, he was ardently in favor of SUDENE. Indeed, he saw in it a most useful instrument for "the redemption of the Northeast." I asked for his present opinion; was he still in favor of it?

"Yes and no," he replied. "SUDENE was a necessity at first, and we, the bishops of the Northeast, are those who were responsible for its creation. We brought about some meetings with government and industrial experts. We helped people see that the absence of any planning structure for the region and the resulting wasteful dispersal of experts and funds could simply not be allowed to continue. This being so, we were and are for SUDENE.

"At one time I believed that SUDENE would manage to change things in the Northeast by creating jobs, by permitting higher wages and thus enable the masses to cease being subhuman and become people.

"But today I no longer have any illusions in respect to SUDENE, which is part of the capitalistic system and without any political possibilities; hence, it cannot redeem the Northeast. Here, as in the rest of Latin America, development can take place only through political action.

"Throughout the Third World, especially in Latin America, government is in the hands of the powerful tycoons, the owners of property. Politics is a world to which the masses have no access. The experts who work in SUDENE know very well that, without a radical structural change in economics and politics, the social and cultural strata, there can be only a development without justice, that is to say, a spurious development. But they also know that SUDENE has neither the right nor the means to bring about this basic structural change.

"On paper, of course, it's a masterpiece, but as I said, and we have the proof, linked as it is with the big proprietors it cannot make the needed structural reforms.

"We have a law of agrarian reform, and it is a good one. We have some organizations to put the law into effect. The Northeast has been given priority in the application of agrarian reform. To ensure greater efficiency, five of these public organizations have merged to constitute GERAN—the Executive Group for the Rationalization of Agrarian Development in the Northeast, it might be called in English. Note this: the second initial letter, E, stands for 'executive.' The five organizations that merged for greater efficiency are the Bank of Brazil, SUDENE, the Institute of Sugar and Alcohol, the Brazilian Institute for Agrarian Reform, and the National Institute for Agricultural Development.

"As a schema, it's perfect. Theoretically the five organizations speaking as one can say to a *senhor de engenho*, a sugar-tycoon, 'We can reorganize your production so that you can produce on a quarter of your lands four or five times what you harvest on your entire domain. On the lands you will no longer need, we could make a real agrarian reform in terms of human development with a program of social, technical, and financial assistance, and so on.'

"Fine! But unfortunately this schema remains on paper. It does not function. And if anyone demands that it function, well, that is called subversion. It's communism! What? You don't respect landed property? We can't believe it. Those are the exclamations of our good Christians for whom property is the greatest dogma, more important than the Holy Trinity, than the Incarnation of the Word. Private property! Which is in fact depriving property.

"For greater security, the powerful landowners have succeeded in obtaining from the government a change in the meaning of 'E' in GERAN. Instead of signifying Executive it now signifies *especial*, or in English 'special.' Because in fact there was no question of putting the plan into execution!

"In the same way, since SUDENE had no possibility of making a true agrarian reform, it had to begin by a plan of industrialization. But since it also had no possibility of basically altering any enterprise, it remains capitalistic, its sole motive being profit, its only problem competition with the industries of southern Brazil and with foreign industries.

"The industries of former times, especially the sugar and textile industries, must modernize themselves. And to the extent that they modernize themselves, instead of bringing in new workers, creating new jobs, they dismiss half their employees— sometimes two thirds of them.

"New enterprises are being set up, it is true, and in great number. But they come with completely modern equipment, half of which is automatic. For example, the Coral Company, which manufactures dyes. It represents an investment of about 10,400,000 new cruzeiros or about $2,342,080. For us, that is a big sum. It is an enormous enterprise, something to marvel at. But when you ask how many workmen that factory employs, you learn that there are exactly—counting the manager and the doorman—just 160 employees.

"SUDENE does the best it can. With the present structures, it cannot go further. And thus, we have a spurious development: the rich become richer, the poor become poorer."

Listening to Dom Helder, I recalled another day when in his laconic yet graphic way he had described the state of things: "In our region," he said one day, "co-exist the early twenty-first century and the twelfth century: the electronic and cybernetic era and the era of feudalism."[2]

Thus, behind the facades of modern factories and behind the bustle of brand new small cars, the official programs and statistics, there is another world and it was that world that concerned the archbishop.

That world can be summed up on an index card: Northeast Brazil: 9 states; 1.5 million square kilometers; 23 million inhabitants; annual income per capita, $100; 70 per cent of the population illiterate; infant mortality, 50 per cent. The largest typical underdeveloped zone in the Western Hemisphere: two humid and fertile strips to the north and east, with their big towns, their shantytowns, their sugar, their capitalism, and in the center the immense arid zone, the *sertão,* the interior, with its cotton, its aridity, its migrating population.

And that world can be read about in books:

The *matuto* (rural laborer) Severino Leite, thirty-eight years old, received me in his house at Campo Grande. It is an adobe house, which is already a kind of luxury, and stands isolated in the midst of rolling lands, cotton plantations, outlined with evergreen hedges. He has seven children still alive and six in the cemetery. His wife offered me a glass of yellowish water, which I politely tasted, for the view of that muddy liquid endows the eye with the keen vision of a microscope, detecting a swarm of harmful animalcules.

In a small enclosure near his cottage, this Severino, a relatively privileged man, keeps a skinny cow. She belongs to his boss, the big landowner. The little milk she gives is for Severino, but the eventual calves and their meat are also for the boss.

A kitchen garden of sorts is in front of the house: it is about two square yards in size. In that plot he raises a few vegetables—not many, for two reasons: the boss's land must produce cotton; and the rural laborer does not much believe in the virtues of fresh vegetables. The garden, so-called, is raised about three feet from the ground on a platform, which preserves it from the ravages of harmful vermin.

Using his *enxada*, the primitive hoe which is still the basic tool of the Northeast cultivator, Severino raises some beans and corn. This year, although there was no real drought, no rain fell in April and May, hence the maize withered and will not produce a crop. Severino especially cultivates some fifteen hectares of cotton, on a sharecropper basis. That is to say, he is lodged in a house belonging to the landowner and has a right to half the earnings on the harvest. Last year the harvest was worth about $515, which meant about $257 for his share. But during the periods of intensive work, he must hire some day laborers and pay them out of his own pocket. And the year before he had had to borrow $200 from the landowner, in order to feed and clothe his wife and children. By the time he paid back that loan, he had $57 left—clearly not enough to keep him going until the next harvest.

When Severino brings his little brood to Mass on Sunday at one o'clock—and the church is a good hour's walk from his house—he is still goodhumored. But not stupid. And when he sums up his condition and that of the landowners, he does so in two expressive words: *escravidão* (slavery) and *urubuzada*, the name of a big bird of prey that leaves nothing of the victim on which it pounces. The economists employ more scholarly terms but it comes to the same thing.[3]

This world of exploiters and exploited is written about in the papers. The "Cabo affair" figured in the news October 1968. A local affair; Cabo is a locality near Recife, where sugarcane is raised. It was, however, a national affair, for President Costa e Silva concerned himself with it, the Minister of Labor sent a delegate to investigate, all the newspapers printed it prominently, raising many questions: would there be a strike or not? Would the strike be legal? Would the police arrest the peasant leaders? Would the peasants have recourse to fire and sword in defence of their rights? And just what did the rural workers' union demand? What they demanded was payment of overdue wages, the distribution of lands in conformity with the law of agrarian reform, and a minimum of social security.

On that last point, I read in a magazine the following disillusioned statement ascribed to the Minister of Labor: "There are thirty-five million rural laborers in the country. The funds set aside for the assistance of these people constitute 1 per cent of the worth of agricultural production, which thus provides 100,000,000 new cruzeiros ($22,520,000); that is, less than 3 cruzeiros per person. State insurance for the rural population is impossible."

At Cabo, where there are twenty sugar-refineries on the banks of the Pirapama River which produce 400,000 tons of sugar annually, there are 30,000 laborers out of work in a town of 60,000 inhabitants. Only one man there has shoes to wear; he is the president of the syndicate, João Luis da Silva, aged twenty-four; they talk about him as of a new Julião.[4] A workman, Manuel dos Santos, lost his arm while employed; he had the luck to be able to return to work as an officer of the union. Thanks to this, he earns 60 new cruzeiros per month—approximately $13.50.

At about the same time there was the affair of the Itaiba parish, whose priest, Father Paulo Santos, threatened with death, had to flee. It was one of those somber affairs of the *sertão*, where water is scarce and where traditionally no stockbreeder can appropriate it. The animals are branded but circulate freely. Well, some of the big cattlemen wanted to increase their stock, so they decided to fence in a sector of the land. The result was the ruin of the small-time stockbreeders, who were cut off from the water. The big proprietors had the mayor and the police in their power, as usual.

In the local newspaper of October 1, I read this statement, attributed to Father Crespo, director of the rural assistance service of Pernambuco: "The climate of persecution existing in Itaiba continues because of the big landowners. They kill the animals of the farm laborers, being unable to kill the laborers themselves, and up to now the government has taken no steps against them." And four days later there was this comment in the *Jornal do Comercio:*

"This is one example of the social problems that arise or are on the point of arising in various sections of the Northeast."

In that same newspaper appeared this true story that I feel impelled to transcribe verbatim:

> A veritable record fast has been achieved in Maceió by young José Saturnino, who went no less than six days without eating, while walking the streets of this capital. Until today, when he fainted in the main street. His condition was so lamentable that he could not move any of his limbs, not even his fingers. Tears had dried on his face and his mouth was open, like the mouth of a lifeless body.
>
> After being taken to the hospital, José Saturnino shocked everyone present by confessing that he was married, was the father of two children, that he had just returned to the North from the South, where he had gone to try his luck in 1962 and having found none returned, only to be robbed of all the savings he had accumulated during his years of work and from the sale of his furniture. A paltry sum: 300 new cruzeiros (about $67).
>
> He also said he had crossed various states, such as Paraná and Minas Gerais, without managing to find any work, until finally he decided to return to Union dos Palmares, in Alagoas, his birthplace. There his wife had fallen ill and he had resolved to leave for Maceió, hoping to find better conditions. When he ran out of money he began to walk the streets, too ashamed to beg and still more afraid to steal, and that is why he reached the condition of collapse they had seen.
>
> He said that when he risked asking for alms, people assumed an air of indifference, told him to go to work, and in an arrogant and self-satisfied way asked him if, with his healthy body, he was not ashamed to beg.
>
> After he had been given care and some money, José had said to everyone that he wanted to find work.

Dom Helder does not read the papers. I told him rapidly this story of José Saturnino. He smiled, and was not amazed. He knew so many other cases of the kind, he witnessed so many others. But he preferred to hear them sung, or to sing them himself:

I am a poor landsman,
I earn my living with my spade.
What I'm paid is shared
with the man who plants nothing.
But to plant for sharing—
No, I'll not do that any more!

Next day Dom Helder launched, in Recife, his nonviolent movement "Action, Justice, and Peace." Two young people had appeared that morning in his house: a young actor who with his company of young people were to put on a play that would show the reasons for and the goals of this movement. Among them was a girl who sang and along with others like her would arouse the crowd with their songs and make them conscious of their destiny. Song and drama: to Dom Helder's mind these say more and with more truth than all the books, all the newspapers, all the speeches.

Zélia Barbosa softly runs through the songs that the audience will take up next evening, beat time to, and applaud. This morning there is no audience except Dom Helder. His eyes sparkle, his hands applaud, he visualizes the world of suffering humanity that throbs in every word. He interprets it[5] for me as the girl sings:

> *If things go on like this*
> *I will leave my "sertão."*
> *Even though my eyes brim with tears*
> *and my heart fills with sorrow,*
> *I will go to Rio and fill the mortars*
> *of the masons in the building trade,*
> *yes, even if God comes to our aid*
> *and rain falls on the "sertão."*
> *But to go on planting for sharing,*
> *no, I'll not do that any more!*

And then it continues with the theme of departure:

> *We'll go away, the ground is dry already,*
> *we'll go away,*
> *we'll leave, no rain has fallen,*
> *we'll go away.*
> *I had such faith in all the promises,*
> *praying to heaven and the saints.*
> *But apparently my voice is dead*
> *for God did not reply.*
> *But better to keep a memory*
> *than to stay here and die.*

And then there's the interminable journey for these jobless on a *pau d'arara*, a "parrot's perch" as they call the jolting trucks with their load of human beings and their belongings. And then the song[6] relates the arrival in Rio or elsewhere, still suffering from hunger, still exiled, and this compounded now with homesickness:

> *Better to return to my Ceará*
> > *for there, at least, I'm someone.*
> *Here I am nothing,*
> > *nothing but a famished creature,*
> > *nothing but a parrot on its perch,*
> > *not even able to sing!*

Departure after departure in hope of arrival:[7]

> *Oh! If to live was to arrive somewhere,*
> > *finally to arrive somewhere,*
> > *stay there and marry,*
> > *marry to send out our children*
> > *into a living world*
> > *and not into such a whirlwind.*

The theme of another song[8] is the earth—the eternal earth that belongs to others, which the rural laborer knows he will never own, except on the day he is buried:

> *That hole in the ground where you lie,*
> > *measured by hands'-breadths*
> > *is the only small profit*
> > *you'll ever get out of life!*

> *It is a good size,*
> > *neither too long nor deep.*
> > *And it is your share*
> > *of this "latifundio."*
> > *It's not too big a hole*
> > *for your miserable remains.*
> > *But you'll be less despised there*
> > *than you were in your lifetime.*

The theme of death is taken up, "dead of old age before you've lived thirty years, killed with a bullet before you've lived twenty, and dead of hunger suffered a little every day."[9] And the resignation—or despair—over the frequent funerals.[10]

Lighting the candles
  becomes habitual,
  the dancing ceases,
  it's disillusion.
Once more a heart stops beating,
  an angel soars to heaven.
May God pardon me
  for it must be said
  the doctor arrived too late.
Because in the "morro"
  there's no car to get into,
  there's no telephone to call
  there's no beauty to see
  and one is dead without wanting to die.

And then it is the theme of life[11] constantly revived. And we
  are with Severino, a child just born:

Severino, you, the migrant,
  let me tell you.
I do not know the answer
  to the question you are asking:
Would it not be better, you wonder,
  to plunge off the bridge of life?
I do not know the answer
  or if you really want to hear it.
It is hard to make a plea for life
  with nothing more than words—
  and still harder when it's the life
  of you, the wretched poor.
But though I cannot answer
  the question you are asking,
  it is life, life itself
  that has replied,
  with its living presence.
And there can be no better answer
  than the spectacle of life:
  to see it unwind—
  that too is life—
  to see the patient working
  of life, it too has work to do,

> *to see it gushing forth*
> *as it gushed forth just now,*
> *in a new bloom, bursting—*
> *even when the bursting-forth*
> *is feeble.*
> *Even when the bursting-forth*
> *is insignificant, as now,*
> *even when it is the bursting-forth*
> *of the life of Severino.*

Severino! Oh yes, Dom Helder knows him well. The very first day Dom Helder arrived in Recife, he introduced Severino to his new diocese.

"Although for some people," says Dom Helder, "it may seem strange, I declare that, in the Northeast, Christ is called José, António, or Severino. *Ecce Homo!* Here is Christ the Man! Man who needs justice, has the right to justice, deserves justice."[12]

"Severino, son of Severino, nephew of Severino has a bleak life, it is a death in life. He vegetates more than he lives a human life. He does not vegetate like a leafy tree, with its roots filled with life, but like the cactus, his brother. Until today, he has not rebelled. He learned from his illiterate parents and at the church of his lordly landowner boss to be patient, like the Son of God, who had endured so much injustice that he died on the cross to save us."[13]

"Formerly, his employers kept slaves, and they managed to make themselves believe that our brothers were happy in their *senzala*, their slavery. Today, Christian employers manage not to see that this slavery continues, even if not so labelled. The workers have the right to die on the land of their masters. They are given shanties to live in with their wives and children. They have work to do for the boss and, nearly always, permission to cultivate for themselves a small patch of land. The employer conscientiously thinks of himself as a good and generous father in his relations with these laborers. And if it is true that the shanty almost never has water or light or privy, the boss pacifies his mind by thinking that God tempers the wind to the shorn lamb.

"The boss considers it his right to pay whatever he wants to, whenever he wants to, since he is already granting a great favor by providing land and house, giving work, and permitting the laborer to cultivate a small patch of ground.

"And if, tomorrow, the laborer shows ingratitude, pretends to be a human being, taking an interest in innovations, frequenting radio schools, participating in trade unionism, talking about rights, then the boss is convinced there is cause for alarm: the wind of subversion is blowing—even, who knows, of communism. And then, without the least hesitation or remorse, he sacks the worker, drives him off his lands, and if need be, demolishes the shanty in which the worker lived with his family."[14]

*   *   *

In 1955, a Recife lawyer, Francisco Julião, began to go up and down the countryside in the Northeast, trying to arouse the peasants from their resigned and fatalistic torpor. Peasant Leagues multiplied and spread. Certain occurrences on the land made people think for a short while that the revolution was beginning. But the leagues were to be dissolved and Julião forced into exile after the "revolution" that was unexpected, the military coup of April 1, 1964.

At about the same time that the Peasant Leagues were being formed, a movement had sprung up and developed that was soon called the Natal Movement. Beginning with a small team of priests interested in studying their common pastoral problems, and a group of the laity convinced that the life of faith demands a minimum of physical well-being, it rapidly mobilized all the energies of the Natal archdiocese, and then extended throughout the State of Rio Grande do Norte and beyond. It was not a "subversive" movement. Instead, it was a powerful awakening of consciences (Dom Helder calls it "consciencization") through basic education, the formation of leaders, the creation of activities and organizations, of cooperatives and unions by means of which the rural laborers would become masters of their own destiny. The big landowners, of course, did not like this calm and dignified popular movement of emancipation any more than they liked brutal peasant uprisings—perhaps less. Their retort was to dismiss, without any preliminary explanation, all the men who had joined unions. But the climate had changed by then. On the plantations, in the villages, commandos were organized in a display of active and massive solidarity of the people with their leaders. The radio of the Movement for Basic Education in Natal broadcast the names of the militants who should be protected. The violent opposition of the landowners to rural unionism was neutralized until, in 1964, it found new resources and new means in the "anti-subversive" apparatus established by the military coup.

Meanwhile, in Rio, the secretary of the Brazilian bishops' conference, Dom Helder, recalled that he was an expert in education. In 1961, in the name of the bishops' conference, he had initiated some negotiations with the government which had resulted in the creation of the Movement for Basic Education (MEB) under the collective responsibility of the bishops and the personal responsibility of Dom José Távora.

MEB is one of the most obviously "revolutionary" enterprises imaginable. True, it merely teaches people to read, but in doing so it opens the eyes of the masses to their fate, to their human rights, and the means they can take to achieve the justice and dignity that are their due. And this, by utilizing all the possibilities of the transistor radio.

In 1963, MEB covered twelve states of Brazil; 7,500 instructors stirred the consciences of 180,000 pupils listening to 15,000 receiving stations in 7,353 schools.

The title of the basic textbook, the *cartilha* (primer), suffices to explain the subjects and objective of this basic education: *Viver è lutar* (To Live Is To Struggle). The peasants not only learned to read in it. They learned, for example, on page 8 that "They work to support the family. But Pedro's family is hungry. The people work and are hungry. Is it just that Pedro's family should be hungry? Is it just that the people are hungry? " Or again, page 62: "The people of Brazil are exploited. They are exploited not only by Brazilians but by many foreigners. How can we rescue the country from this condition? "

Some time before the coup d'etat of April 1, 1964, the powers of the established order saw the danger represented by MEB. In February, Carlos Lacerda, governor of Guanabara (State of Rio) had the "subversive primer" seized. "If this primer is not an instrument of a people's revolution and propaganda for communism, I don't know what it is," Professor Gudin wrote. "I must say that the positions taken by this Communist wing of the Catholic Church, to which Archbishop Távora has allied himself, are the result of an ignorance particularly inadmissible on the part of those who pretend to teach others to read." To the mind of Professor Gudin, declaring, as the primer did, that "every human being has the right to a dignified level of life" was "a proposition worthy of an ass, because absurd."

The episcopate itself became split on the subject. According to the papers, Cardinal de Barros Camara, archbishop of Rio, made it known that he "had nothing to do with the primer ordered by MEB."

When the military came to power in April 1964, their first action was against MEB, against its militants both priests and laymen, against the Catholic Action movements such as the JUC (Juventude Univérsitaria Católica) and the JOC (Juventude Operária Católica)[15] in which the leaders had seen the natural extension of their evangelical commitment. Everyone who thought and could help others to think was censured, exiled, or imprisoned. Alceu Amoroso Lima talked with reason of "cultural terrorism." And three years later, Dom Helder could still clash with a regime whose "mistrust of intelligence, of criticism, and of freedom to think and create" stifled all chance of vitality: "We will achieve no economic development in a climate that maintains and aggravates intellectual underdevelopment.[16]

A muted struggle then began from the north to the south of Brazil, between the power of the government and its henchmen on the one hand, and on the other the forces of conscience which included the conscience-awakeners, among whom Dom Helder at first played a star part. He was no longer secretary of the bishops' conference and thus could speak out. But very soon Dom Helder was not alone. With him, enlisted in the struggle, were other bishops, collegially sustained by the regional bishops' conferences and even by the national conference.

The new order—moral, military, and capitalistic—was not twelve days old when Dom Helder presented himself to his diocese with his program. Everyone understood his meaning when he said, "We must not think that the problem can be restricted to a few little reforms, and we must not confuse the fine and indispensable concept of order, which is the aim of all human progress, with certain caricatures of it, which are responsible for the permanence of structures that, as everyone knows, cannot be preserved." And again, when he said, "We must not be afraid of having clear ideas, even if we repeat them: development signifies the awakening of consciences, of public opinion, and of culture, and personal advancement and technological planning.[17]

Three days later, April 15, 1964, Dom Helder and seventeen bishops of the Northeast appealed to the government, demanding that "the innocent people who were imprisoned in the confusion of the first moments be given their liberty, and that even the guilty be treated with the respect due to all human beings."

Next day the troops of the Fourth Army invaded the Episcopal Palace of Recife. Naturally, Dom Helder protested.

In July, Dom Helder held a press conference.

"For how long," he exclaimed, "will this self-serving belief last that everything good for the people is tinged with communism?" And he dared to insist that "without reforms it is impossible to surmount the obstacle of underdevelopment. The bishops' conference has proclaimed this repeatedly, and the reforms cannot be postponed. . . . Without agrarian reform, the almost inhuman misery of the rural workers will persist. Without banking reform, little will be done for the development of the country, and without fiscal reform, the rich will continue to grow richer while the poor will continue to suffer. Without electoral reform, the elections will appear to be free but in fact will be subjected to the power of money. Without administrative reform, bureaucracy will continue to sap the strength of public life."

What business had a bishop of the Church to interfere like this in the affairs of state? On May 2, 1965, Dom Helder explained himself publicly. The occasion was furnished by the inauguration of the regional seminary of the Northeast, at Camaragibe.

"This establishment," he said, "will prepare priests for preaching the gospel. But you cannot evangelize abstract creatures, intemporal, existing in a void. When our seminarians get to the churches and chapels and speak of divine grace, that is to say, the presence within us of the Holy Trinity, of the grace that enables us to share in divine life, how can they forget that they are proclaiming divine life to listeners who very often live in subhuman conditions? . . . To persist in a purely spiritual evangelization would soon result in giving the impression that religion is something separate from life and powerless to touch it or overcome its absurd and erroneous aspects. It would even tend to support the view that religion is a great alienating influence, the opium of the people.

"Thus, the humanization of the people can no more be isolated from evangelization than it can be confused with it. . . . We, the bishops of the Northeast, are convinced that we should foster rural unionism as the only practical means for the rural workers to claim their rights from their overlords. . . . If we feel obliged not simply to hand over to the laity an endeavor that would normally be the domain of these Christians in temporal matters, it is because we consider it necessary to give moral support to the elementary defense of human rights, given the blind and heartless abuse of authority by some of those 'overlords.' And if certain people have the audacity to pin the label of Communist even on the bishops of Holy Church who devote themselves to the eminently Christian mission of defending abused human beings, what will become of our priests and especially our laymen if we abandon them to their fate?"[18]

This address made a "painful impression" on the editor in chief of the big capitalistic newspaper, *O Estado de São Paulo*, who found in it a great many "statements, each one of which is more deplorable than the others." There followed an inflated polemics. Inscriptions bloomed on the walls of Recife. Dom Helder was treated as "an illiterate" and as "the unconscious tool of the Communists." Good Christians wrote to the nuncio expressing their indignation with the new archbishop. A few movements of solidarity with "the Red Archbishop" formed, nonetheless, especially among the student population of Recife and São Paulo.

The tension increased in 1966. On March 31 of that year, Dom Helder refused to celebrate a Mass for the second anniversary of the so-called revolution. "It is not a question of a religious ceremony," he wrote, in an explanatory letter to the commander of the Fourth Army, "but in fact a civic-military meeting with political overtones."

On July 14, Dom Helder signed, along with other bishops of the apostolic region of the Northeast II, a manifesto supporting Catholic Action (ACO, Acão Católica Operária) and rural Catholic Action (JAC) and their recent denunciations of unjust structures of government and society. The army general forbade the diffusion of this manifesto.

At the beginning of August, circulars were sent out from the military headquarters in Ceará, addressed directly to all the priests of the Northeast and bypassing the bishops, denouncing Dom Helder explicitly as "a left-wing agitator," accusing him of "always stirring up ideas that stir up people." The conflict was now an open one: who would win?

August 13, the president, Castelo Branco, had a talk with this troublesome archbishop of Recife. August 17 it was learned that the army general responsible for those circulars was to be shifted to another post. And in fact he was.

Meanwhile, in Recife, the commander of the Fourth Army was replaced by General Souza Aguiar, an old friend of Dom Helder. Dom Helder was not present at the ceremony of his installation, but had a cordial meeting with him six days later, August 29.

However, the affair was not over with, and according to rumor the government intended to ask Rome to transfer the archbishop. Hence, the importance accorded by public opinion to the audience granted by Castelo Branco to the nuncio, Archbishop Baggio, who declared, "The religious-military conflict in the Northeast is the result of misunderstandings, which we are trying to dissipate." Later on the nuncio made another statement: "It is a duty of Catholics, whether organized or not, to support the activities of their pastors." Hence, too, the importance accorded to the manifestations of solidarity with Dom Helder expressed by many bishops from the north to the south of the country. More equivocal seemed to be the support that came from the opposition party, the M.D.B. (Movimento Democrática Brasileiro). The Minister of Foreign Affairs, Juracy Magalhaes, was to be received by the pope September 13, and on January 6, 1967, the pope was to receive Marshal Costa e Silva, president-elect of Brazil.

Dom Helder was not transferred.

On August 21, the great writer, Gilberto Freyre, violently attacked Dom Helder in the press. He recalled his past as an "Integralist" and compared the archbishop to the famous Nazi at the head of political propaganda who had mastered some efficacious techniques. Then, the writer went on, "this Brazilian Goebbels, pale, ascetic, intense, eloquent, gesticulating, theatrical," and, comparing him to Kerensky, sneered, "There are some in foreign milieus who would like to see Dom Helder president of the republic of Brazil, which would then give us a Brazilian Kerensky."

Dom Helder replied on August 26, and Gilberto renewed his attack two days later. Dom Helder had other things to do than engage in an interminable polemics, so fell silent.

Some weeks later, October 5, it was learned that the bishop of Campos, António de Castro Mayer, had addressed a letter to his brother bishops, following the manifesto of the bishops of the Northeast. In this letter he expressed anxiety over a language that risked having grave consequences "for a country that desires to repel communism in a decisive way." The manifesto, he wrote, "does not avoid favoring in a certain way the creation of the materialistic and egalitarian mentality advocated by Marxist socialism." It "showed no fear of the benefit that the Communists—who were always stirring up the class struggle—might eventually derive from such language."

This theme was to be amply taken up again and orchestrated in the following months until, in 1968, an archbishop, Geraldo de Proença Sigaud (of Diamantina) was to clamor everywhere and in every tone of voice, an alert against "the Communist infiltration" in the Church, designating Dom Helder Camara by name, with the result that, also in 1968, the movement "Family, Tradition, Property" was able to mobilize 1,500,000 signatures to a petition asking the pope to carry out a serious purging of the Church.

It would take more than all this to keep Dom Helder awake at night or to stop him from talking and acting. In April 1967, he lent all his support to a violent and precise indictment by the ACO of the Northeast, in a manifesto entitled "Development without Justice!"[19]

On June 21 he was invited to speak at an informal meeting held in a private room at the Chamber of Deputies in Brasilia, under the auspicies of the Institute for Research on Brazilian Reality. He seized this opportunity to denounce Yankee colonialism and the viewpoint of those who were leading the government to hand over Brazil to it.

"Let us be finished with the illusion that we can overcome underdevelopment," he said, "by accepting aid which has proved to be deceitful and even antiproductive; let us align ourselves resolutely with those who demand a complete reform of international commerce.

"Let us be finished with the false dichotomy of capitalism versus communism, as if the fact of being in disagreement with capitalistic solutions implied adherence to communism, and as if to criticize the United States were synonymous with a liaison with Russia or Red China."

With facts and figures in hand, he demonstrated that Brazil had practically surrendered to North Americans the control of her educational program, from primary school to college.

"Is there any other nation in the world," he asked, "that is so completely alienating itself in a domain as vital and sacred as education? We will never attain a harmonious and responsible civilization at the price of the spiritual annihilation of one people by another."[20]

Another opportunity was offered him to speak out plainly, when on September 25, he was made honorary citizen of Pernambuco. The commanding officer of the Fourth Army could not tolerate this speech, which also aroused protest in the municipality of Recife. Dom Helder called to mind a great hero in the struggle against African slavery in the nineteenth century:

"If tomorrow Joaquim Nabuco were to come to Recife and were to visit, for example, our sugar production zone, would he not feel impelled to renew the abolitionist campaign? How would he react to the wages so often withheld? What would he say to the suppression of paid vacations, the suppression of 'the thirteenth month,' and even the annulment of guarantees, and the absolute hopelessness with which the people of our countryside face the daily tasks that are manifestly beyond their strength? Would Nabuco believe that there are still employers who forbid the workers to go to school or join trade unions?"

Dom Helder was becoming dangerous to those in power. Already, in June 1967, the great writer Gustavo Corção had suggested that the pope should bestow upon him not an eventual cardinal's hat, but a straw sombrero with two holes cut in it for his ass's ears. Now, in November, the ex-minister Raimundo de Brito noted that "the clergy of Pernambuco, Paraíba, and Rio Grande do Norte are arousing anxieties in the entire region with their distorted interpretations of the encyclicals. The priests of the Northeast do not go in for religion, but for politics." And as to the government deputy, João Calmon, "the capacity for proselytism of Dom Helder and the priests under his authority is infinitely greater than that of Miguel Arraes and Julião before March 31, 1964."

A book could be made with nothing more than the articles published day after day attacking Dom Helder, perhaps even with nothing more than the articles against him published by Vanderkolk Wanderley, municipal councillor of Recife, who seemed to have as a profession the unmasking of the archbishop as an agent of international communism.

And yet, attacked, denounced, threatened, Dom Helder remains there, unchanged. Visibly he is afraid of no one, especially unafraid of the ruling power, civil or military.

He does not even falter at the possibility of arrest, a lawsuit, or imprisonment; he simply could not, it would be impossible.

From where does he draw his strength? From where does he draw his confidence? One cannot help but suspect, to begin with, his political ability. For one recalls his past, is acquainted with his ease in mingling with the great, no matter what their political color. Did he not meet with President Goulart a few days before his fall, and then with Marshal Castelo Branco, the number one "anti-Goulart man"? It is interesting at this point to reread this comment he made in an interview for *Fatos e Fotos*, June 1964, on the declaration made by the episcopate, thanking the so-called revolution for having warded off the Bolshevik peril:

"Some people are astonished that governments come and go while the Church always maintains her attitude of collaboration. Well analyzed, this attitude merely proves that the Church is bound to no one . . . but maintains an attitude of respect, always ready to help and serve the people, whether the president is called Vargas or Cafe Filho, Nereu Ramos or Kubitschek, Janio Quadros, João Goulart, or Castelo Branco."

After Castelo Branco there was Marshal Costa e Silva. At that time Dom Helder declared to Marcel Niedergang, who was interviewing him for *Le Monde:*

"If the Costa e Silva government manifests real signs of democratic goodwill, I consider that we ought to encourage him in that direction. We should aid him. It is the hope of all Brazilians that the successor to Castelo Branco will adopt a new line. Let us give him a little time to go into action. If nothing happens, nothing changes, then we shall revise our position. We will be the ones who will change."

Dom Helder poses a problem for me. How can a man who is a priest combine in himself all the violence of a prophet with all the subtleties of the politician?

When I put these questions to him, Dom Helder replies by first excusing himself.

"I ask you to forgive me, because I perhaps give you the impression of being more a politician than a bishop or a priest. But in present world conditions, to be preoccupied with human problems is as though commanded by the Gospel." He then went on to explain: "During these past twelve years I have forced myself to maintain good relations with the public powers. That is to say, I have continued to engage in dialogue with the successive presidents of the Republic, from the dictator Vargas down to the present time. In 1955, for instance, we organized more than one ministerial meeting presided over by Vargas and then by his successor, Cafe Filho, to examine the possibilities of a collaboration by all the ministers in the preparation of an international Eucharistic Congress. I maintained the same attitude under the government of Kubitschek, then of Janio Quadros.

"I recall, for example, the very interesting encounters between the bishops and technicians who organized SUDENE in the Northeast. The president of the Republic came for the winding up of those sessions. And I remember the contacts with Janio Quadros, who was a rather special president, during the creation of the Movement for Basic Education.

"After that, there was João Goulart, who was a bourgeois more than anything else. He was rich. But he had a certain sensitivity when it came to the problems of the people. He spoke openly in favor of reforms. But in order to have the backing he needed, he gave the impression of leaning to the left, of going perhaps a little too far. He believed that at a certain juncture he would be able to dominate the situation.

"I know that some people say that Dom Helder, as secretary of the Brazilian bishops' conference, was too closely allied with João Goulart. In particular there was a photo in the newspapers just four or five days before the coup d'etat—or the revolution—which, in 1964, was to overthrow the Goulart government. It showed the president of the bishops' conference—at that time, Cardinal Motta of São Paulo—in the company of President Goulart and me.

"At the time, I gave no explanation of that photo, because Goulart's government had fallen. But God knows the reasons that had brought us together!

"Goulart wanted, at that time, to make the revolution, and he relied, on the one hand, on the army, and on the other hand, on the Brazilian C.G.T. (Comando Geral do Trabalho). He had made a speech that already sounded the call for revolution in the streets; he had made that speech surrounded by army sergeants.

"Early next day I telephoned Cardinal Motta. 'Your Eminence, I have something to tell you,' I said, 'and have some suggestions to make. May I take the plane to São Paulo?' He replied to this by saying, 'Perhaps you and I are concerned about the same thing. I was just getting ready to leave for Rio, to speak with you.'

"When he arrived, we saw at once that we did share the same concern. How could we open João Goulart's eyes? How make him understand that the army sergeants he expects to support his revolution are, in a way, the underdeveloped elements of the army? It needs but a command from a captain and instinctively the sergeant obeys. A sergeant is loyal to his captain, not to the revolution. Not to mention the Brazilian C.G.T.! We have no real tradition of trade unionism here. The only trade union in Brazil was given to us by a dictator. There is no real trade union experience. On nhe contrary, we have had the experience of what is called *peleguismo*: when the president or the leader of a union has some courage and ideas, he is considered by the government to be a Communist and is replaced by a puppet, a *pelego*.

"Thus we were worried about the same thing, the Cardinal and I. And I immediately telephoned to President Goulart. 'Cardinal Motta and I urgently want to speak with you,' I said. The president invited us to lunch, insisted on it, assuring us that no one else would be present. He said there would not even be a waiter to serve table. Everything would take place in his private study.

"And indeed the interview started just as the president had promised. But then he committed an unexpected act of betrayal: the door opened and without warning a photographer took that famous photo. Had Goulart remained in power, I would have told this story to explain what some people have tried to present as proof positive that the Church was in collusion with that government. But since his government fell, I remained silent. I do not like to speak of those who cannot give their own explanation.

"And thus it was that, as secretary-general of the bishops' conference, and in a situation more or less normal for this country, I forced myself to maintain relations with the public powers.

"Since the coup d'etat of April 1, 1964, it has become a different matter; I am no longer a diocesan bishop among others, in a zone where the misery of the destitute is terrible. Perhaps I am mistaken, but I still feel that this coup d'etat was made, whether consciously or not, for the benefit of the big tycoons and landowners. It is true that the army was afraid of communism. It is true that with Goulart communism may have had some chance of acceding to power.

"Today, I never make personal attacks against the president or against anyone. It is none of my business. I am even convinced that the best of presidents, the best of governors could not do very much within the structures we have. Instead, I try to induce everyone to work toward the overthrow of those structures.

"I had some contacts with Marshal Castelo Branco. He is a native of my own part of the country, Ceará. While his wife was still alive, both he and she listened to and watched my radio and television programs in Rio de Janeiro. Then, Castelo Branco was personally convinced that I was not a Communist. And since we were both from Ceará, he has spoken with me directly in especially difficult moments. He would telephone and say, 'Let us have a talk together like simple natives of Ceará.'

"The first time he did this, after April 1964, I remember very well. When we were alone, I said, 'President Branco! Today I woke up rather anxious. Because I discovered that I have a left hand, a left leg, a left half of my body. I am anxious, because I see that today it is very dangerous to be on the left! And now I discover that you, too, President Branco, have a left side. Now really, this is ridiculous!'

"Yes, I have kept open this possibility of talking with politicians.

"And let me tell you this: God knows, I do not recall ever having, at any time, gone to visit or talked to a president of the Republic without remembering that I am a bishop. I was always present as a man of the Church. I very well remember that one day President Kubitschek wanted me to be mayor of Rio de Janeiro. He had asked me before that to be Minister of Education. And afterward, Janio Quadros wanted me to be vice-president. But I always replied without the least hesitation, 'No, no, and no! I am a man of the Church. I am here to serve the people, and what I can do as bishop I could never do if I agreed to follow a political line and accepted a government position.'

"In the past there were priests who engaged in politics. Today it seems clear to us that politics is rather the affair of the laity. For example, I recall what I said to Kubitschek: 'President Kubitschek, we are personal friends. But when we meet I never forget that I am in the presence of the chief of state. And I believe that you always recall that you are confronting a bishop of the Church. That is to say, we can talk in a normal and friendly way. But if tomorrow I come to you in the role of mayor or minister, then I am your subordinate. And above all, I would be linked to a political party. And I remember my youth and my youthful sin.'

"I refer to my association with the Integralists as a sin, because I believe that everything that happens to us has a providential meaning. The two years I spent as a member of the Integralist party, well, it's as if my heavenly Father had wanted to vaccinate me against politics!

"I quite often listen to what people say. 'To save this country, we need a new president of the Republic!' But never, never again will that arouse in me even the beginning of a temptation.

"However, I am persuaded that the Church, in Latin America, can still be of service to the people. And so, for the moment—I can say this to you and other Europeans especially—I am making the most of a certain clerical advantage. There! That is what I am doing! Because, in this country today and in present conditions, a bishop can say what a student or workman or an intellectual, even a professor, could not risk saying."

N O T E S

1. Address on the occasion of the installation of Dom José Maria Pires, archbishop of João Pessoa, March 26, 1966. *Cf. Revolução dentro da Paz*, Rio: Sabia.

2. "I Am the Way," address at the inauguration of the Theological Institute of Recife, March 7, 1968, unpublished.

3. Cited in *Informations Catholiques Internationales*, December 15, 1963, from Collard, *NEBRA* [Northeast Brazil]: *un effort exemplaire de développement régional*, Mons (Belgium): Dimanches, 1963.

4. See p. 39.

5. "Peasant's Fate," by João Donvale.

6. "Parrot's Perch," by Vinicius de Morais and Carlos Lyra.

7. "Arrival," by Edu Lôbo.

8. "Funeral of the Sharecropper," by João Cabral and Chico Boarque.

9. "Life and Death of Severino," by João Cabral and Melo Neto.

10. "Lighting the Candles," by Ze Keti.

11. "Life and Death of Severino."

12. Address delivered April 12, 1964, upon taking possession of the archdiocese of Olinda and Recife. *Cf. Revolução dentro da Paz* and *Le Tiers-Monde trahi*, Paris: Desclée.

13. "Science and Faith in the Twentieth Century," address at the School of Polytechnics, Campina Grande, December 17, 1966. *Cf. Revolução dentro da Paz*.

14. Address at the School of Law of the Federal University of Rio Grande do Norte in Natal, December 8, 1966. *Cf. Revolução dentro da Paz*.

15. These are Brazil's form of the international "specialized lay apostolate" movement which has developed from the original Jeunesse Oeuvrière Chrétienne, founded in Belgium in 1925 by Joseph Cardign, and its extension to students. In the United States the terms are Young Christian Workers (YCW) and Young Christian Students (YCS). —ED.

16. Address at the Institute for Research on Brazilian Reality, Brasilia, June 21, 1967.

17. See above, Note 12.

18. Address at the inauguration of the regional seminary at Camaragibe, May 12, 1965. *Cf. Revolução dentro da Paz* and *Le Tiers-Monde trahi.*

19. The complete text of this manifesto was published in *Le Tiers-Monde trahi.*

20. See above, Note 16.

Don Quixote Rides Forth Again

If there are hare-brained streets
unable to preserve a secret,
arrogant streets
that preen themselves
on the glories of their past,
there are also old dead-ends
that silently preserve
the simple joys they've witnessed,
and the anonymous virtues
that have sanctified their humble stones.

RIO, JANUARY 15, 1953

3

"I trust you enough to suggest that, in each country in Latin America, the hierarchy, without in any way neglecting its directly pastoral work, . . . should give its moral support, if need be, to a nonviolent movement in every country that would be capable of prodding the big landowners who are still living in the feudal style of the Middle Ages."[1]

I do not know why some commentators have felt they could explain Dom Helder Camara's vocation for nonviolence, which was particularly expressed in 1968, by supposing that he was acting on instructions received from Paul VI in Rome during April of that year. Certainly he must have been given a confirmation of his views and even emphatic encouragement. But from the year 1965 at least, the archbishop of Recife had already dreamed, imagined, desired to do what he was to attempt three years later.

The Council was drawing to an end. In two successive press conferences, Dom Helder said "what the Council could not say" and expounded what, in his opinion, "a postconciliar period worthy of Vatican II" should be, which was "to examine, in the light of the Council, directives on war and peace, and given the particular conditions of Latin America and some other experiments carried out in other parts of the world, if need be, whether or not to stimulate a nonviolent action as an arm of peace in the underdeveloped countries."[2]

This idea, this project, was to mature and become more explicit in the following months. We need but note a few of his statements on the subject:

"Urgently needed is a worldwide campaign for the abolition of present-day slavery, in order to complete the political independence of nations by an economic independence accessible not only to a few privileged classes or a few isolated regions, but to the entire population. It is high time that Don Quixote rode forth again."[3]

And again, in the following year:

"The social revolution that the world needs is not an armed coup d'etat, is not guerilla-fighting, is not war. It is a profound and radical change which presupposes divine grace and a transformation of public opinion which can and must be aided by the Church of Latin America and of the entire world."[4]

And still later in that same year:

"Am I abusing my privileges as sponsor when I invite you to join, this very day, a movement that is free of partisan, denominational, and racial restrictions, a movement that is radical in its objectives and democratic in its methods, and will lead to a creative revolution that can well be called 'Development and Humanism'?"[5]

And two months later:

"The great question we must ask is whether the social revolution, which the whole world needs, can be achieved by education, or whether it will come about through violence and armed conflict." To this rhetorical question he replied: "Anything that is accomplished without educative work, without preparing minds to accept it, does not take root. A transformation misunderstood by those who are forced to make concessions will bring nothing but bitterness and resentment. . . . It is a dream hard to realize but I hope realizable, my dream of creative revolutions that will bring about radical and rapid changes."[6]

In this brief resumé of Dom Helder's consistent advocacy of nonviolence, we have reached the threshold of 1967. Camilo Torres had died in the previous year, fighting in the Colombian maquis, or guerilla warfare. His heroic choice of violence had become exemplary for a number of altruistic souls. In Bolivia "Che" Guevara and his guerillas, the arrest and trial of Régis Debray, had mobilized public opinion. There was a growing impatience with and mistrust of any movement that could divide and disarm the revolutionary forces. And Dom Helder spoke out:

"This cannot be achieved with movements that are supertimid and supercautious, proceeding with solemn slowness. Without audacity and grandeur, one cannot take hold of a continent."[7]

In 1968, Dom Helder had made his decision: Don Quixote was definitely riding forth once more. In his many conferences in

Brazil, Berlin, Strasbourg, and Paris, he proclaimed his decisive option for nonviolence:

"Allow me the humble courage of taking a stand: I respect those who have felt obliged in conscience to opt for violence, not the facile violence of armchair-guerillas, but that of the men who have proved their sincerity by the sacrifice of their lives. It seems to me that the memory of Camilo Torres and Che Guevara deserves as much respect as that of Dr. Martin Luther King. I accuse the real abettors of violence, all those on the right or on the left who wrong justice and prevent peace.

"My personal vocation is to be a pilgrim of peace, following the example of Paul VI. Personally I would prefer a thousand times more to be killed than to kill anyone.

"This personal position," Dom Helder explained, "is founded on the Gospel. . . . We need only to turn to the Beatitudes—the quintessence of the Gospel message—to see that the option for Christians is clear. We, as Christians, are on the side of nonviolence, and this is in no way an option for weakness and passivity. Opting for nonviolence means to believe more strongly in the power of truth, justice, and love than in the power of wars, weapons, and hatred."[8]

It was then that Dom Helder laid the foundations of a real movement. In the United States, Martin Luther King had just been assassinated. The archbishop of Recife took up the torch of active nonviolence.

He surely must have read and reread the "commitment pledge" that Dr. King had demanded of his blacks. It derives from a situation that is not that of Brazil and from a personality that is not that of Dom Helder. But we can see in it the spiritual roots of an option for nonviolence that represents an attitude and a morality rather than a political line:

> I hereby pledge myself—my person and body—to the nonviolent movement. Therefore, I will keep the following Ten Commandments:
>
> 1. Meditate daily on the teachings and life of Jesus.
>
> 2. Remember always that the nonviolent movement . . . seeks justice and reconciliation, not victory.
>
> 3. Walk and talk in the manner of love, for God is love.

4. Pray daily to be used by God in order that all men might be free.

5. Sacrifice personal wishes in order that all men might be free.

6. Observe with both friend and foe the ordinary rules of courtesy.

7. Seek to perform regular service for others and for the world.

8. Refrain from the violence of fist, tongue, or heart.

9. Strive to be in good spiritual and bodily health.

10. Follow the directions of the movement and of the captain on a demonstration.

In the same document where Dom Helder reproduces this "pledge," he sums up both the presuppositions and the objectives of a nonviolent revolutionary movement:

"A threefold mutation of mentalities (cultural revolution in a new sense) is a fundamental necessity in our case, as preliminary to the profound and rapid changes we want to achieve:

"It is urgently necessary to sensitize the powerful so they will of themselves decide to give up their privileges, and also to sensitize Latin American governments so they will decide to bring about the basic reforms.

"It is urgently necessary that young people try to discover adequate solutions to our real problems.

"It is urgently necessary that we aid the masses to become a people."

Dom Helder had already forecast the dates for the initiation of the movement: October 2, 1968, to show that what was possible for Gandhi, whose hundredth anniversary would begin that day, was not impossible for Brazil and for the Third World; November 2, to extol the memory, among all the dead, of those who were victims of the fight for liberty and justice; December 10, to make people realize that the rights of man, solemnly promulgated by the United Nations twenty years previously, were far from being respected.

Already, too, Dom Helder had counted the forces that could be mustered: 15 per cent of the bishops would try to enlist 15 per cent of their priests who, in their turn, would try to mobilize 15 per cent of their most devout parishioners. This was one of Dom Helder's key ideas. "Today, as always," he said, "humanity is led by minorities who hope against all hope, as did Abraham."

Whereupon Dom Helder set out to find his ardent episcopal minority.

Nineteen bishops of the various South American countries, who comprised the Department for Social Action of CELAM, assembled from May 12 to 19 at Salvador da Bahia. "Together we traced the main lines of a peaceful action," says Dom Helder, "which goes much further than the texts: the important thing is to discern the moral pressures that could instigate the basic reforms, while avoiding dangerous recourse to armed violence."

In July, the National Conference of Brazilian Bishops (CNBB) assembled in Rio. Dom Helder found a name for his movement: "Moral Pressure for Liberation." Forty-three bishops out of the two hundred and fifty-three at the conference—or more than 15 per cent—signed the pact:

> "We, the bishops of Brazil, moved by the love of God and of our fellow men; conscious that we owe a longstanding debt to the Latin American peoples; desirous of collaborating in the liberation of millions of the children of God who, in our country and on our continent live a marginal life, economically, culturally, artistically, politically, socially, and religiously; feeling that only a clear and positive, courageous, and coordinated action will give practical consistency to such documents as the Constitution on the Church in the Modern World and the encyclical on the Development of Peoples, and to the conclusions reached at Mar del Plata.[9]
>
> "We hereby do affirm our resolve to stimulate to the maximum Moral Pressure for Liberation with its initial program of stirring the consciences of people as to the fundamental rights of man, by putting the accent on liberation from all forms of slavery or servitude (art. 4 of the U.N.'s Universal Declaration of Human Rights), on the right to life, liberty, and personal security (art. 3), and on work (art. 23).
>
> "We desire to receive suggestions and material from the coordinating center of Moral Pressure for Liberation, the implementing of which will be committed to our care.
>
> "Our signature to this document has the value of a pact."

The information center mentioned was established in Recife. From that center issued first a *Caderno No. 1*, which defined Moral Pressure for Liberation, its evolution, its methods of action, its immediate program. In this "notebook" we read the following declaration of principle adopted successively by the Social Action Committee of CELAM and by the Conference of Brazilian Bishops:

"Within the context of Latin America, nonviolence must be expressed by an attitude of nonconformity in regard to the established injustices that exist under diverse forms and pretexts. This nonconformity will manifest itself in a courageous and constant functioning to obtain thorough, urgent, and daring structural reforms as rapidly as possible, to meet the demands of justice. For lack of this, sooner or later violence may become inevitable and in fact is one of the temptations at the present moment."

The center then issued a *Caderno No. 2* on the rights of man with, for each of the three articles on which attention was most particularly focused, some suggestions for the required awakening of consciences (what Dom Helder always calls "conscientization").

A *Caderno No. 3* followed, on Gandhi:

"How think of the liberation of the Brazilian and Latin American masses in terms of moral pressure without having loom up before us, as inspiration and example, the liberator of India?" Dom Helder had learned from Gandhi, "respected by all religions as a saint," two lessons: "That we too should have the courage to aim at the liberation of everyone and from every kind of imperialism that weighs upon us; changing from one imperialism to another does not solve the problem.

"And also, in speaking of liberation from the exterior forces that constrain us, we should always keep in mind that the beginning of beginnings is the inner liberation. How can one who is himself a slave liberate others?"

Dom Helder had also learned from Gandhi the efficacious methods of nonviolence, from the boycott or strike, to fasting. But there was no question of flatly copying, without making the necessary adjustments, no question of becoming a vegetarian, of going on hunger strikes. What Dom Helder feels can be learned from him is the spirit of nonviolence. The first lesson learned is that he who conquers himself is the only one who can be victorious, that he who frees himself is the only one who can free others. It is the teaching, viable in all times, that the authentic nonviolence (not the false, cowardly, and hypocritical nonviolence) is stronger than violence and hate.

Caderno No. 4 gives some specific suggestions for the application of the stated principles. Dom Helder, in this "notebook," insists on the need for personal commitment. Just as the coordinating center keeps a register of the bishops who, with full knowledge of the facts, sign the "pact," so each of those bishops should keep a register for the signatures of his priests, and each priest should keep a register for the signatures of his faithful.

"To assert," writes Dom Helder here, "that the pact will frighten and that without it the movement would have many more adherents is to misunderstand that one of the fundamentally distinctive characteristics of moral pressure resides in that very adhesion. It is a movement of people who are thoroughly convinced, who are resolved to take the consequences of their convictions. In a time when violence exerts such a serious and grave attraction, we must know how to win free minds without any reservations, but courageously and lucidly making a choice while aware of all the risks of being misunderstood and condemned. How, otherwise, could we hope to win over such people?"

The calendar that had been set up was followed. On October 2, 1968, the movement was launched; on November 2 and December 10 there were demonstrations. These first clashes with public opinion had to be very carefully prepared and discussed in groups; someone had to be found who could back them up in the town and state assemblies and even in Brasilia; they had to obtain sure means of publicity in the newspapers and magazines, on radio and television programs, had to find if possible some schoolmasters who would let their pupils participate, with competitive essays on Gandhi, on various martyrs for freedom, and on the rights of man, and had to enlist the cooperation of musicians, caricaturists, and actors or singers.

The lines for concrete action had to be drawn up before November 1968 and a program for 1969 had to be settled. Each group and each person in the groups was asked to send in ideas and suggestions. From then onward it was a question of working most particularly on the rights of man. This had to be done on every level, by means of exact investigations of current conditions, and was to mobilize the greatest possible number of inhabitants and experts. "If we want to make the rights of man cease to be merely a phrase, we must constantly place the theory in juxtaposition with the reality surrounding us," wrote Dom Helder.

The "concrete suggestions" were merely suggestions. Dom Helder did not want to force things; he wanted the movement to remain open and adaptable to changing conditions. Nor did he want to impose his personality upon the movement. He was aware of what could be contributed to the movement and what had already been contributed by the ideas and energies issuing from the specialized Catholic Movement for a Better World [10] and the joint pastoral plan. He even approved the idea of some laymen in São Paulo who wanted to find a wider range of activity by setting up a "fraternal movement" less clearly defined and less solidly committed to nonviolence, a "Collective Action for Justice," as they called it. He wanted each bishop who had signed the "pact" and each group to retain freedom of action.

Dom Helder believed that before the movement could be more firmly established it should first experiment, feel its way. Perhaps the crucial moment would come in July 1969, at the meeting of the Brazilian bishops' conference. Afterward they would need to prepare a coordinated structure on a continental scale, since at the assembly of the bishops at Medellín it had barely been outlined.

But that "afterward" had already begun. When Dom Helder was invited to Berlin, Paris, Dakar, New York, Munich, Manchester (in the U.S.A.), St. Louis, or elsewhere, he immediately saw a providential occasion to mobilize the "violence of peaceful people" even in the developed world.

Dom Helder finally gave me *Caderno No. 5* in which he explains the new name of the movement: Action, Justice, and Peace. The denomination "Moral Pressure for Liberation" had aroused unfavorable reactions. "Pressure" frightened people, and clearly it is better to disturb people with the fact of what one is rather than with the banner under which one appears. The expression "moral pressure" recalled to some people the phrase "Moral Rearmament." And so, to avoid creating this confusion the name was changed.

At Medellín, in Colombia, in September 1968 the second meeting of the Latin American bishops' conference (CELAM) was held. Dom Helder at once got down to business there: his hand is easily seen in the conclusions on justice and peace. After some exchanges of viewpoints with the bishops of the various Latin American countries, he focused attention on a rough draft of regulations, which clearly stated just what the movement was on the eve of its being set in motion:

Action, Justice, and Peace, has as its goal the humanization of all those who are subhumanized by misery or dehumanized by egoism. And it will achieve this by means of:

(a) The gradual but effective and rapid change of socioeconomic structures and political and cultural structures throughout Latin America.

(b) Latin American integration, without imperialistic meddling either external or internal. This integration should begin by the integration of all the people in each country.

Action, Justice, and Peace is interconfessional and is open to all who care to join in.

Action, Justice, and Peace comprises and practices nonviolence as a positive action, daring and courageous assertion of nonconformity in regard to the present structures of Latin America.

The universal Declaration of Human Rights, still so far from being applied in Latin America, sums up the fundamental principles of Action, Justice, and Peace.

As sources of inspiration for this movement we wish to mention notably: the pastoral Constitution on the Church in the Modern World and the encyclical on the Development of Peoples, as well as the conclusions reached at the second meeting of the Latin American bishops' conference, particularly concerning peace, justice, youth, education, the poverty of the Church, and the apostolate to the elite and the masses, and at the assembly of Uppsala promoted by the Ecumenical Council of Churches, and at the reunion "Church and Society" at Geneva.

In every country, according to circumstances, the movement Action, Justice, and Peace will endeavor to:

(a) Arouse and encourage evaluative groups, preferably interdisciplinary, with the aim of studying specifically the various methods for rapid development which can be adapted to our several countries.

(b) Study the concept and the methods of nonviolent action.

(c) Study the existence or nonexistence of conformity or nonconformity and the practical distortions of the laws relating to reform of structures, always taking into account the particular needs.

(d) Eliminate obvious injustices, such as conditions of slavery, collective dismissals of workers in rural or urban zones, sub-subsistence wages, lack of respect for the rights of man, especially in regard to the less favored classes.

(e) Denounce the armaments race, which divides the nations, wastes national resources, and prevents any authentic integration.

(f) Denounce violent action against all justified demonstrations which do not disturb the public order but which are often arbitrarily declared illegal.

(g) Denounce national and international monopolies and every advance of imperialism.

(h) Be attentive to every kind of development that takes place to the detriment of man.

Once the thought of the evaluative groups has matured and the option for nonviolent action has been defined through personal commitments, many ways will occur for putting into effect the objectives of Action, Justice, and Peace. For example:

(a) Meetings for awakening consciences that are well organized and well constructed and led.

(b) Intelligent use of the means of social communication, through music, drama, and caricature.

(c) Support for justified strikes.

(d) Big demonstrations or marches, as the culmination of some well-organized activity.

(e) Peaceful demands, even at the risk of imprisonment, in defense of those who may be unjustly arrested for defending the values we proclaim: this is one of the fundamental forms of nonviolent action.

On October 1, the eve of the launching of the movement Action, Justice, and Peace, Dom Helder was, as always, serene. At his home, there was a constant procession of journalists, local, national, international. To each one he tirelessly repeated the same thing, always with the same conviction. Tracts were circulating in town: "Come, see the devil and protest!" read one. From where did these tracts issue? One hesitated among three hypotheses: perhaps from the right-wing movement "Family, Tradition, Property," which sees Communist subversion everywhere; perhaps "Popular Action," a radical revolutionary movement which perhaps wished to seize the occasion of provoking disturbances that would develop in chain-reactions. Or perhaps from the army and the police, who wanted the masses to be so afraid of street-incidents that they would stay indoors. This little guessing game explains the climate of that day.

How many people would come? It was clearly impossible to engage in a big propaganda campaign. The local capitalist press restricted itself as always to the minimum of information imposed by the competition of the Rio and São Paulo newspapers.

In any case, the impression of a mass rally must be created, and Dom Helder found it. He had retained a small assembly room that could accommodate only three or four hundred people, at the São José school run by nuns, situated in the big avenue, Conde de Boa Vista. If there were more people, then the meeting could be held in the large courtyard that separates the school from the avenue.

That big patio was to prove to be too small to accommodate the three thousand or so people of every condition, secular and religious, who crowded there at nightfall. And a small crowd, at least as animated as the large crowd, filled the harshly lit balcony: actors, singers, newsmen, some nuns, some priests. In a corner, back to the wall, Dom Helder stood, quivering with excitement, contributing his presence to the action. For action it really was: this initiating of the movement was not an academic session but was, in the strict meaning of the word, a demonstration.

A company of young actors spoke and sang a poem by Vinicius de Moraes which evoked the plight of workers in the building trade. Beneath the balcony, facing the crowd, placards were raised:

ACTION, JUSTICE, AND PEACE; REVOLUTION WITHOUT VIOLENCE; AGAINST ESTABLISHED VIOLENCE; LAST LEGAL RECOURSE; WE DEMAND AGRARIAN REFORM; AGAINST POLICE BRUTALITY.

Another young theatrical company presented the aims of Action, Justice, and Peace in spoken chorus, with interludes of popular songs. The audience responded to each phrase:

"Peace is our ideal. Not merely any peace, not a false peace, but the true peace that Christ brought to the world.

*"A swamp seen in moonlight can deceive the onlooker.
It gleams like a vision of beauty; but underneath there is
nothing but filth and ferment.*

"We do not want the peace of swamplands, the deceitful peace that conceals injustices and rottenness.

"*There are people who are greatly concerned with maintaining law and order. They have no fear of an apparent law-and-order that deserves the name of disorder and undermines peace.*

"*Forty-five million Brazilians—half the population—do not have 36 new cruzeiros (about $8) a month to live on or make some semblance of living.*

"*To trumpet this truth is not to be against true order or true peace. It is to be in opposition to the appearance of an order and peace which are preparing the explosive uprisings of the future.*

"*To trumpet such truths is not to be against anyone in particular. If half of our population does not have 36 new cruzeiros a month to maintain a minimum livelihood, it is to some degree the fault of everyone.*

"*Out of 100 Brazilian families, 70 do not receive even the minimum wage.*

"*And among those who receive the minimum wage, many receive it only on paper.*

"*What can the head of a family do, with five dependents to support, even if he earns the supposed minimum wage?*

"*Must we conceal the fact that out of 100 Brazilian families, 70 do not receive the minimum wage? Must we conceal the fact that the house is burning, or is it not better to know it and to try to put out the fire?*

"*There are appearances of order and peace that hide terrible injustices and undermine peace.*

"*The National Housing Fund builds thousand of houses throughout the country; but that National Fund does not risk losing its money. It has no thought of lower-income housing except for those earning one or two minimum wages.*

"*The 70 families out of 100 who do not even receive the minimum wage can only look on at a distance, can only sniff the fragrance of the house being built by the National Housing Fund.*

"*Is it subversion, is it communism, to open people's eyes to these truths?*

*"The working class knows better than anyone, suffers in
its flesh the hard truths that many, quite naively, would
prefer to conceal.*

*"Let us pause for a moment to recall the songs that all Brazil sings,
and which prove that the people are conscious of the injustices
they endure.*

The assembled crowd then raised its voices in the night, singing the songs we quoted in an earlier chapter. Then the speakers
took up their story.

*"These misfortunes and others endured and sung by the people are
caused by the unjust structures that must be changed without
delay.*

*"What is this mystery? Money has been allotted to the
Northeast, new enterprises abound here, yet unemployment increases, as do hunger and misery!*

*"What is the melancholy secret of the rich who become richer
while the poor become poorer?*

*"The melancholy secret is the fact that business con-
siders money (or capital) more important than work;
that is to say, more important than mankind.*

*"Business enterprises that put profit above everything else must be
changed; undertakings that appreciate the expensive machine more
than the man in charge of the machine, but who is cheap and
replaceable, must be changed.*

*"As the thirst for profit is insatiable, the machine be-
comes ever more powerful and constantly takes over
more and more of man's work. There is constantly less
need of the man.*

*"We are not opposed to progress. But we want progress to serve
everyone, not merely a group that is constantly smaller and richer.*

*"The workman must be master of his work. It is not
enough that he should earn a good wage. To work is an
essential need of the human being.*

*"The human being cannot be sold, nor can he sell himself. All
buying and selling of work smacks of slavery.*

"What is the melancholy secret of so much misery in the

rural world? What is the melancholy secret that obliges millions of God's children to live in subhuman conditions, a species of slavery?

"The agrarian structure must be changed.

"Pope Paul VI has well said, 'The earth was given to all, not merely to the rich.'

"Surely this is not communism. It is the voice of the pope.

"We have no objection to the ownership of private property, provided that everyone can own property.

"Private property that deprives the many can no longer be allowed. Private property cannot be allowed if it deprives others of the necessities of life, of what a man needs if he is to support his family respectably.

"But, you will say, do we not have a law of agrarian reform in Brazil? Do not the Northeast zone and the zone of sugar refineries have priority in the application of that agrarian reform?

"Yes, there is a law of agrarian reform and there are a number of organizations to implement it. But there is no change in political structure.

"The great masses of landless people do not know how to read and cannot vote. The powerful are masters of the political structures and do not allow the application of the laws that affect their privileges.

"Until the government builds grammar schools, high schools, and colleges, this condition will endure.

"The poor register their children in a school, wanting to see their children have more advantages than they have had.

"But then, they take their children out of school and put them to any kind of work that will help conquer hunger.

"Without a change in the structures of industrial enterprises, without a change in agrarian structures and political structures, there can be no reform in education.

"University reform in 90 days is nothing but a joke!

"Schools must change. We want schools that free every-one from slavery.

"We want schools that free everyone from the slavery of igno-rance, unemployment, hunger, and fear.

"And there is the slavery of superstition, discourage-ment, fatalism, egoism, sin: schools should free mankind from this.

"The present structure encloses human beings in the way that a shell encloses the chick. Water strikes hard stone until the stone is pierced. With one peck of the beak and another and another peck, the chick manages to get out of the shell.

This was a session of conscience-awakening and we were right in the midst of it. The themes and the terms were simple, ranging from one elementary evidence to another. The diction was on the borderline between recitative and chant. The phrasing was rhythmical. The crowd applauded, whistled, repeated the phrases, commented on them.

Dom Helder was still leaning against the wall. He knew the text off by heart. All his ideas, all his revolutionary mannerisms were there, as was all his past as judge and expert in education, and these ideas poured out in a cascade of vivid words that went straight to their mark.

"We are often asked if we believe that our movement Action, Justice, and Peace is logical in expecting that a change of structures can be made without violence.

"And Action, Justice, and Peace replies with another question: Do you remember that the all-powerful slave-owners in Brazil were unable to prevent the 13th of May?[11] A certain May 13 saw the triumph of the idea of truth and justice that had been preached far and wide by young ideal-ists.

"We are completing what was accomplished on that May 13 by now seeking the liberation of native-born slaves.

"In 1888, the slaveowners had everything in their power: pride, force, the press, the desperate passion of people defending their own fortunes and destiny.

"And young idealists such as Castro Alves, Ruy Barbosa, and Joaquim Nabuco kindled the hearts and minds of others, without killing anyone, without resorting to violence, and stirred them to such an extent that a moment came when all resistance was unavailing.

"Here and now the youth of the country are ready to overthrow, if possible by peaceful means, the old structures and build new ones.

"The first to align themselves with us, as our natural allies, are the rural and urban workers. They are the main victims of today's injustices. They want to free themselves from the *peleguismo* and they are ripe to aid in the task of awakening consciences.

"The leaders of all religions cannot but take an interest in our cause. What religion does not fight for peace, and what religion does not realize that, without justice, peace is illusory?

"The press, communications both printed and spoken will surely be with us.

"But do not these communications endure the control of economic power?

"There are idealists on the staff of every newspaper, every magazine, every radio and television station. And if our endeavor makes news, even if only because of economic interests, it will be talked about.

"The technicians will be with us. More than anyone, they know we are in the right.

"Very often the technician is obliged to earn his living and realizes he is imprisoned within the actual structures. Distressed, the technicians will aid us as much as they can.

"The artist is with us; he is our man. He has a sensitivity and suffers over the injustices of the world.

"Even among top executives of business enterprises we have some allies. And those who run medium and small industries are all too well aware that they are being devoured by the international trusts.

"It would be a gross error to neglect politics and politicians. To be afraid of soiling our hands by involving ourselves in politics is to act like Pharisees.

"What would become of our country were we to abandon politics to the incapable or the dishonest?

"Now is not the time to go into details, but it is time to ask the question:

"If the African slaves in Brazil were emancipated thanks to the enthusiasm of Castro Alves, Ruy Barbosa, Joaquim Nabuco, why cannot we, all united, succeed in peacefully overthrowing the old structures and laying down new foundations?"

The evening was wearing on. But there was still a very good long speech on Gandhi. The crowd, one felt, was becoming overwhelmed with discomfort and fatigue. Dom Helder, still but a discreet shadow on the white wall, showed in the expression on his face all the variations of the crowd's emotions. When at last it came time for him to speak, he needed but a minute, three phrases, to reestablish contact, revive attention and enthusiasm. He became one with the audience. The loud, warm, impassioned voice that issued from his frail body filled all space:

"Already violence is installed in Latin America: the violence of small privileged groups that maintain thousands of God's children in a subhuman condition. Superficial reforms are not enough.

"Many Latin American governments, sometimes unknowingly and without wanting to, are preparing the explosion of the worst of nuclear bombs, worse than the A-bomb: the M-bomb, the bomb of misery.

"The M-bomb is being prepared by those who are afraid of our efforts to arouse the masses to an awareness of their misery and try to prevent it under the captious accusation, the captious and from now on ridiculous accusation of subversion and communism.

"The M-bomb is being prepared by those who try to repress by force the protests of the young, of the workers, and even of the Church, to the extent that the Church feels it her human and Christian duty to lend a voice to those who cannot speak.

"Our movement of Action, Justice, and Peace recognizes that, if need be, armed revolutions which break out or will break out in the future can and could be considered as wars of liberation.

"And our movement of Action, Justice and Peace was not conceived as a movement that should attempt to subdue the 'No' of the oppressed but instead to aid in giving to that 'No' the effect of a universal 'No,' courageous and positive, beautiful and constructive.

"Action, Justice, and Peace was not conceived as a dull and dismal movement, tolerated and tolerating. We know that God rejects the dull and tepid. Our movement aspires to be and with God's help will be the violence of the true lovers of peace."

Dom Helder proceeded to describe the objectives and methods of the movement, taking up again the terms of the preliminary regulations that had been elaborated at Medellín. The crowd was with him, showing by its clamor that it agreed with the orator and was thinking of the menace hovering at that very moment over the workers in Cabo.[12] Especially when Dom Helder emphasized that "to denounce the violence exercised against just causes, even if they are mistakenly declared to be illegal" was a violence to which the movement was opposed, and declared that "everything that is legal is not necessarily just, so long as the laws of man do not respect justice to mankind!"

But now that Action, Justice, and Peace had been set in motion, what was there to do?

"Some people will ask how to join the movement. Can one join now, or can a group join en masse, enlist now, in public?

"Action, Justice, and Peace is not interested in enlisting new members hurriedly, under the stress of emotion. Today we are asking for no new commitments. From tomorrow onward, anyone interested in the movement can join a team of at least five, at the most fifteen, other persons equally interested in joining the movement. Anyone who does not want to make the effort of finding five to fifteen comrades or who would be incapable of acting in a team should renounce coming with Action, Justice, and Peace.

"However, any interested person who can think of a number of people who would join with him in the movement, can leave a list of those people with their addresses.

"There will be a course of instruction, followed by the signing of a pact for those who decide to join us."

After saying this, Dom Helder gave three addresses where next day the lists of candidates could be left.

"How many will we be? What will we be worth? What results will we manage to obtain? How will we proceed? Will we not be ridiculously helpless against the impregnable walls of the unjust old structures that must be overthrown? Shall we be able to replace with something valid the unjust structures we destroy? Shall we not be blowing up a balloon condemned to collapse next day? Shall we not, in short, be outdone by the violence brought against us?

"Let me reply to these and other questions by reminding you that God exists, that he continues to exist and will always exist. And his determination will always be to punish the proud and exalt the humble.

"In the struggle between David and Goliath, who would have wagered on that boy-shepherd pitted against the giant Philistine who, in fact, was brought down by a slingshot and five stones. Our five stones are: faith in God, confidence in truth, confidence in justice, confidence in the good, confidence in love!"

Thus was begun a new chapter of the already long and always difficult history of nonviolence, on October 2, 1968, at Recife with Dom Helder Camara, and simultaneously at Barra do Pirai, Victoria, Campina Grande, João Pessoa, Goiania, Santos, São Paulo, and other Brazilian towns whose bishops had signed the pact.

Next day, recollecting that evening session, I could not help but call to mind constantly a short phrase of Dom Helder, words that might be the beginning of a great story, coloring it with a tinge of mocking skepticism: "It is high time that Don Quixote rode forth again." When I told Dom Helder this, he was not at all shocked.

"I see," he commented. "You see, I am very fond of Don Quixote. He is much more realistic than is generally believed. When I face a crowd of people as I did last night, I have the impression that my talk about overthrowing structures without armed force is, for a number of the young, quixotic. And yet there is realism in it, I might say political realism."

"Many think and say," I responded, "that your movement will die before it is six months old, either stifled under the violence of the wealthy or overwhelmed by the violence of the poor."

"Yes," said Dom Helder, "there's some logic in what you say. But I don't think it's an affair of only six months. I believe we'll have more time. But it's true that if our movement is to make its way, it will create problems with the governments, with the great powers. On the other hand, I have no illusions. If we remain timid and lacking in courage, if nonviolence is not understood and practiced as a positive and courageous action of nonconformity with the unjust status quo, then there is the risk that we will be outdone and left behind by some of our friends who have chosen and will choose to use violence.

"To take a great example: I think that Martin Luther King died at the right moment. Had he not fallen then, he would have been overrun and outflanked by his blacks. He had already begun to be outdone."

"Isn't it the normal risk every educator takes?" I asked: "He provides the minds of his pupils with weapons and stimulates their resolves, only to see them elude his control?"

"That's the argument military men always use when trying to convince me that I'm a subversive and a Communist. They tell me, 'You, personally, are a good man. But it's easier and quicker to arouse the consciousness of the masses, to open their eyes, much easier than to carry out reforms. If you go on waking up the masses,' they say, 'then you are preparing the revolution! You are a subversive. You are playing the game of the Communists!' To this I make my reply. 'You are under a delusion,' I tell them, 'you think that if the Church refrains from opening the eyes of the masses, the eyes of the masses will remain shut. But they will not. Whether with us or against us, their eyes will be opened.' And when occasionally someone tells us that the Church is moving too quickly, my opinion is that we are four centuries behind. We accepted African slavery. Oh, I know: the epoch wanted and condoned slavery and I don't believe I am either more clairvoyant or devout or Christian than my forebears were. No doubt, had I myself lived in that period I would have accepted the institution of slavery. I might even have owned slaves; it was done in that era. But the plain truth is that we did accept the slavery of Africans for three whole centuries.

"Well, I ask you: what could a priest say at Mass in 'the big house,' confronting the Savior and confronting the slaves? He preached patience, the acceptance of suffering along with the suffering of Christ. I know that these are great virtues. We will always need patience, and it will always be very important to offer our sufferings in union with Christ's suffering. But within that framework, the Church played the game of the oppressors.

"After the abolition of black slavery, we continued and still continue to accept the enslaving of the native-born. That is why we must carry out this work of waking up the masses, even though we are aware of the risks."

"But," I said, "Action, Justice, and Peace goes further than merely opening the eyes of the oppressed. Do you really have faith in nonviolence?"

"To begin with, let me tell you why I have no faith in violence. I have two reasons. As I constantly repeat, I am quite aware that already, in Latin America, violence is established. Because, if a quite small minority exists whose wealth is based on the misery of a great number, that is already violence. But if we caused a war of liberation to explode, it would immediately be crushed by the imperialistic powers. Powers, in the plural. The United States cannot accept a second Cuba in Latin America, its sphere of influence. And Soviet Russia would obviously come immediately. And Red China and Cuba.

"Ever since the small attempts at revolution in Bolivia and Colombia, there are military bases everywhere in Latin America, capable of crushing every sort of guerilla warfare. The strength of the guerilla fighters was in training their men in regions where modern armaments are completely meaningless. But today, at the antiguerilla bases, soldiers are being trained precisely for those infernos, those inaccessible regions. I was in Colombia and I saw, in regions that were formerly the domain of the *guerilleros*, an antiguerilla base where, for example, the soldiers let themselves be bitten by snakes in order to be vaccinated and prepared for no matter what test.

"In the case of Brazil, particularly, it is all too clear that there are powers that have not the least interest in seeing this giant, too weak at present, become a real giant tomorrow.

"That is my first reason. I have no interest at all in causing a war to break out, even a war of liberation, if I am convinced that it would be immediately crushed.

"And I have another reason. The revolution will not be fought either by the students or the priests or the artists or the intellectuals; it will be fought by the masses, the oppressed, and they will be the victims of that repressive action of the powers.

"Well, I am in direct contact with the masses and I know that underdevelopment, both physical and material, unfortunately carries with it a spiritual underdevelopment. There is a discouragement, a lack of reasons for living, a fatalism. Why die? Very often in Latin America the masses have risen in revolt only to die and cause others to die. But they know all too well that the great of the world may change among themselves, but as for the oppressed, they always remain sunk in misery. They have no real reasons to live.

"It seems to me that in the next ten or fifteen years there will really be no possibility of mobilizing the masses for a war of liberation.

"I respect and shall always respect those who, with a clear

conscience, have chosen or choose or will choose violence. I do not respect the drawingroom-*guerilleros*, but the real ones. Yes, I respect them. But since they recognize that there are no real chances for violence in the next ten or fifteen years, I tell them, 'Then give me that time. I am going to make an experiment.' "

N O T E S

1. "What the Vatican Council Could Not Say," press conference in Rome, November 24, 1965. *Cf. Le Tiers-Monde trahi.*

2. "A Postconciliar Period Worthy of Vatican II," press conference in Rome, December 1, 1965.

3. Concluding address for a course organized by ECLA [the U.N.'s Economics Commission for Latin America] at Salvador, August 24, 1966.

4. "The Active Presence of the Church in the Development and Integration of Latin America in Light of the Principles of the Second Vatican Council," report prepared for the CELAM meeting at Mar del Plata, October 1966. *Cf. Revolução dentro da Paz* and *Le Tiers-Monde trahi.*

5. "Development and Humanism," address at the School of Economics, Belo Horizonte, December 13, 1966. *Cf. Revolução dentro da Paz.*

6. "Education for Change," address at Princeton University, February 10, 1967. *Cf. Revolução dentro da Paz.*

7. Address at a congress of M.I.J.A.R.C. [Movimento International de Juventud Agrária y Rural Católica] in Asunçión, August 2, 1967, unpublished.

8. "La violence: option unique?" conference given in Paris, April 25, 1968. *Cf. Informations Catholiques Internationales,* May 15, 1968, and *Le Tiers-Monde trahi.*

9. CELAM met there in October 1966 on the theme, "The presence of the Church in the development and integration of Latin America."

10. A movement founded in Italy in 1952 by Riccardo Lombardi, S.J. It has an international center at Rocca di Papa, Rome, and centers and houses in various countries, including one in Recife.—ED.

11. Slavery was abolished in Brazil on May 13, 1888.

12. See pages 32-33.

Spokesman for the Third World

No one has comprehended
how earnestly I've wanted
with my own hands
to relieve the weary horse
of its harness and its saddle
and its blinkers, most especially.

But I know that I have done so,
praying for more than half—
much more, much more than half
of loved and destitute humanity.

RIO, OCTOBER 1950

4

"It is for the Third World, it is for you that we have done this! Come to bear witness for us!"

I have already told how "the nine of Baltimore," the nine American priests and laymen who, in protest against the war in Vietnam had made a public auto-da-fé of the draft cards they had taken from a recruiting office, had called upon Dom Helder for aid, on the eve of being brought to trial. And I have told how seriously Dom Helder had taken this appeal.

Behind the walls of their prison, had those nine American Christians thought of appealing to the pope to testify for them? Or to Cardinal Roy, president of the Pontifical Commission for Justice and Peace? Or to Cardinal Alfrink, international president of the movement Pax Christi? Or to the secretary-general of the United Nations, U Thant? Or to Bertrand Russell, that great private judge of crimes against humanity? Or to some Nobel Prize winner? Perhaps, but I do not know. What I do know from the person concerned is that they turned to the little archbishop of Recife in Brazil, a town most Americans never heard of.

Dom Helder, spokesman for the Third World. How did he get this reputation? He has never spoken from the rostrum of the United Nations. He has never haunted the corridors of the United Nations or lobbied there, in behalf of trade and development in the Third World, nor at Geneva in 1964, nor at New Delhi in 1968. His participation in the Conference *Pacem in Terris* at Geneva in 1967 was not particularly outstanding, and in the previous year he had not been in New York. He has never even flown over Asia. His first contact with Africa was in December 1968, at Dakar, thanks to an international meeting of Catholic jurists.

And yet, when Editrice P.I.M.E. of Milan brought out a collection of some of his writings and addresses, they chose for the title *Terzo Mundo defraudato*, which was reprinted by Desclée in France as *Le Tiers-Monde trahi.*

It is always a question of how we use our eyes. Dom Helder sees far beyond the limits of his direct experience. He has the eyes of a poet, of a prophet who reads the analyses of a Father Lebret with the eyes of a Teilhard de Chardin and who interprets the pontifical encyclicals in the fiery language of a Saint James. Some slight and elementary indications in the newspapers are enough to put him in communion with the world.

He is not an economist, but he denounces the iniquitous laws of international commerce. He is not a jurist, but he demands the internationalization of the American antitrust laws. He is not a political pundit, but he condemns both of the political blocs that share between them the planet. He has never been in the Soviet Union or in China or Cuba, or in any socialist country, but he makes careful assessments of the many experiments that attempt to set themselves up as models for the Third World.

Are his visions hastily improvised? Are his judgments over-simple? Are his slogans banal? Specialists think so, either ironically or with annoyance. To them, Dom Helder is no more than a barroom strategist who enthralls loafers with his easy solutions to every problem, solutions that appear to be sensible but wouldn't work. Some people even reproach him for diverting the minds and energies of his listeners from the serious analyses which alone could lead to useful options and actions.

Dom Helder is sensitive to the objections, because he is sensitive to incomprehension. He is aware of his incompetences and respects competence. He does not want to pose as someone he is not. But he wants to be true to what he is.

"In no respect do I pretend to have the key solution," he tells me. "I am seeking it. I am not an expert, either in economics or sociology or politics. I am a pastor and I see my people suffering. And so I reflect, I try to find a way, I ask for the collaboration of those who can think."

As a matter of fact the situation is clear and simple: on the world-scale as on the scale of Brazil, unjust structures make the rich become always richer while the poor become always poorer.

Dom Helder has read the report of the Argentine, Raul Prebisch, secretary of the Commerce and Development Conference established by the United Nations. It sums up conditions at the mid-point of the decade for development promulgated by the U.N. for the period 1960-1970, and what that report divulges is catastrophic.

In five years the developed countries had seen their gross receipts rise from $1,400 per individual annual income to $1,700 (+ 21 percent), while in underdeveloped countries individual annual income rose only from $132 to $142 (+ 7.5 per cent). The increase in agricultural production everywhere came up against out-of-date agrarian, financial, and commercial structures. In the 1930's, the underdeveloped countries could export 11 million tons of cereals; today they have to import 30 million. The developed countries more and more manage to do without the raw materials furnished by the Third World. For example, from 1957 to 1961 they had to import 27 per cent of the cotton they required; in 1965 the amount had fallen to 17 per cent. The developed countries have imposed higher duties on the manufactured products imported from underdeveloped countries than on those from other countries: 17 per cent on the average as compared with 11 per cent. The balance of payments in the underdeveloped countries is falling dangerously. In 1948 they could cover 70 per cent of their imports; in 1965 they could cover only 30 per cent. The U.N. had asked the developed countries to assure the underdeveloped countries an annual financial aid equivalent to a minimum of 1 per cent of their gross national product. That minimum has never been reached. In 1964 the total debt of the underdeveloped countries reached the sum of $38 billion with an interest of $4 billion.

And what else? According to official statistics, the United States, between 1950 and 1961, exported capital to the sum of $13.7 billion; during the same period, its earnings amounted to $23.2 billion, a "suction" of $9.5 billion. From 1950 to 1961, North American credits in the Third World increased by $22.9 billion; during the same period, the decline in the flow of raw materials caused a loss to Latin America of $10.1 billion.[1]

Dom Helder has a more personal and less bleak way of presenting the same picture.

"When we become fully aware of the fact that a minute portion of humankind exists which, by its technological advances, moves farther and farther away from the remainder of forgotten mankind living in subhuman conditions in matters of comfort and well-being, we have cause to be alarmed.

"When we are confronted with the evident absurdity of that minimal portion of humanity divided into two power-blocs—apparently ideological, but fundamentally motivated by economic interests—manipulating the underdeveloped world for their own benefit, tranquility, and expansionist aspirations, with no real interest in our underdevelopment, we are saddened.

"When the underdeveloped world comes to realize that those two power-blocs have entered a costly armament race, a race that permanently endangers the fate of humanity on earth; when the underdeveloped world finds out that the 'aid' received from those two power-blocs is devoid of meaning in relation to the deterioration of the prices set on its raw products, there is reason to be greatly concerned.

"When the underdeveloped world takes note that its desire for a thorough and rapid renovation of the socioeconomic structures which keep it in poverty is opposed by one or the other of those two power-blocs as being 'subversive and Communistic' and sees that it is being exploited by one or the other power-bloc eager for new satellites; and when the underdeveloped world perceives that its wars and revolutions are decided or immediately exploited by the two power-blocs, then—

"Then education for development has attained, in the underdeveloped world, dramatic proportions and characteristics."[2]

Were it not Dom Helder speaking, one might be surprised that such a tirade could lead to a program of education. One is reminded of a "Che" Guevara, who was impelled by the same analysis of conditions to foresee twenty Vietnams being started in Latin America and elsewhere, which would exhaust both the Pentagon and Wall Street, those two pillars of American imperialism. One thinks of a Sukharno, of a Nehru or a Nasser who, in 1955 at Bandung, had begun to shake the foundations of established hegemonies and disturb the consciences of those in power. One thinks of a Fidel Castro, whose revolutionary tricontinental conference constitutes in a way the final expression, politically and culturally, of the Third World's determination to impose respect for their right to exist as free and sovereign nations.

We know Dom Helder and know that he no more refuses to the poor of rich nations than to the poor of poor nations the right to resort to legitimate defense against their aggressors, and is aware that the eventual violence of the poor should be blamed upon their aggressors. Let us recall that he was the first to sign the

"Message of Some Bishops of the Third World" published at the height of summer in 1967. He signed that message, which is at the same time an appeal: "It is a subversive war that money has craftily waged for a long time throughout the world, massacring entire nations. Now it is time for the poor, abetted and guided by their legitimate governments, to defend efficaciously their rights to life." He knows that the poor can expect nothing from the generosity of the rich. In that same message, we find: "The poor of the poor nations and the poor of the rich nations, amidst whom the merciful Father has placed us as pastors of a small flock, know by experience that they must count on themselves and their own strength more than on the aid of the rich. Yes, certain rich nations or some rich people of certain nations do grant an appreciable aid to our peoples; but it would be a delusion to expect a spiritual change in all those who, as Father Abraham warned us, 'will not be convinced even if someone should rise from the dead' (Luke 16:31). To begin with, it is up to the poor nations and the poor of all nations to accomplish, by themselves, their own betterment.' "[3]

Dom Helder and the other bishops who signed the "Message" might have added that poor nations, like the poor of rich nations, neither should nor can hope for rehabilitation from their governments, even legitimate governments, for those governments are all too often merely docile instruments in the hands of the great powers.

Hence, for those who believe neither in the possibility nor the efficacy of wars of liberation, and for those who do not believe in the representativeness or determination of those who govern the exploited people, there remains no other solution or hope but in education, in the awakening of minds and in favoring and mobilizing the living force of those peoples so they will finally give themselves governments sufficiently strong and representative to make themselves heard in the concert of nations. If the goal is a worldwide government endowed with the necessary means to define the elementary laws of international justice and make them be respected, the movement to attain that goal can only begin from "the bottom."

"No one is under the illusion that there is or could be an authentic dialogue between the super-strong and the super-weak," said Dom Helder at the closing session of a course given in August 1967 by CEPAL (the U.N.'s Comisión Economica para América Latina) at Fortaleza. But that dialogue between the developed world and the underdeveloped world is, for him, "*the* dialogue of the century." But it is unthinkable in the present world situation.

"I dream of a Latin American integration," he confided to me, "confronting the capitalistic empire which is headed by the United States, and confronting the Socialist empire, which is headed by Soviet Russia, and confronting the Common Market. The nations of South America must draw together, must become integrated. But not in the way that Latin America has up to the present carried out integration. I dream of an integration that will accept neither external imperialism nor internal imperialisms.

"There is a certain kind of integration that plays into the hands of foreign imperialisms. Take, for instance, the common market of Central America: it is perhaps more dangerous than no common market at all, for it appears that those countries, which expended such great efforts to achieve integration, have ended up by being placed more submissively within the orbit of the United States.

"And there is also a certain kind of integration that would play into the hands of the mini-imperialisms of the continent. Unfortunately, egotism is a terrible force. Even an underdeveloped country such as Brazil, which has begun a small development, is already behaving in a mini-imperialistic way toward weaker countries such as Paraguay and Bolivia. We have crushed the Paraguayan textile industry. We must therefore be very careful: Latin American integration, yes; but without mini-imperialism, whether Brazilian or Argentinian or Chilean.

"For the moment, it is unthinkable. Just about everywhere in Latin America the military is in power, and military men have their own peculiar philosophy. Take for example the philosophy of the Brazilian military academy. It is public, its books are open for all to read, so I am betraying no state secret. It seems to me a rather weak philosophy. It is based on the conviction that a third world war is inevitable and that the United States will emerge victorious. But even were the United States to win that war, it could only survive a modern war in an exhausted condition. Conclusion: Brazil should fight beside the United States in the war, with the assurance that with the United States emerging exhausted, the new great power would be—Brazil! With such ideas, it is impossible to talk about continental integration.

"So strong is the egotism of our Latin American nations that without the moral aid of the Church they will never agree to the concessions indispensable to integration.

"But if the Church can help the various Latin American countries to achieve a true national integration first of all, and then a continental integration, I believe we would have some possibilities."

Dom Helder sees far into the future.

"Even though the developed countries are beginning to do without certain of our raw materials, they still do need some. Well, if the continent becomes integrated it could say, 'No raw materials will be exported from now on from this continent without some preliminary processing,' and this would have some effect. It's incredible that we should always have to sell our raw materials at the lowest price and then buy industrial products at constantly higher prices. The developed nations of the world do not seem to understand that in their relations with the underdeveloped world there is a problem of justice, and not merely a problem of aid."

Long before Paul VI proclaimed the facts in the encyclical on the Development of Peoples, Dom Helder had adopted its main principles.

"You know better than I," he said to an audience in 1966, "that the most serious economic problem of our time is the urgent need to study the relations between the developed nations and the underdeveloped nations. As long as the developed nations think in terms of 'aid,' as long as they are not convinced that it is a question of justice on a worldwide scale, there cannot be an understanding among the peoples nor will there be peace on earth because, without justice, peace is impossible."[4]

And on another occasion, he said, "What we need is to be rid of the illusion that we will emerge from underdevelopment through the sort of aid that has already proved to be deceitful. Let us stand firmly beside those who demand a complete reform of international commerce."[5]

"My idea," he explained to me, "is by no means to set Latin America apart as a new power-bloc to confront the other superpowers. My idea is always of a universal solidarity: friendship between the too-powerful and the too-feeble is impossible.

"And I never think of Latin America otherwise than in collaboration with Asia and Africa. We owe an enormous debt to Africa, and may also have responsibilities in regard to Asia and its human problems.

"I recall the impression I had when the new independent African nations sent their first delegates to the United Nations. Obviously I was glad to see the young blacks who arrived as ambassadors. When they figured in photographs with the other delegates, those from the United States or the Soviet Union, they could believe and make others believe that they were with equals. Well, I felt like saying to them, 'Oh, my brothers! In Latin America we have had more than a century of political independence. And because of our experience we can tell you that political independence is worth almost nothing without economic independence.'

"I recall, too, how shaken I was when, at Bandung, Africa and Asia decided to try to advance together. If you look at Asia or Africa or the two together, you see a Babel of nations confronting imperialism: a Babel of languages, cultures, races, religions. There is an enormous distance between one region and another, between one country and another. On the other hand, Latin America is nearly unified by language and religion, and has experienced political independence for more than a century. Latin America is remarkably well constituted for sowing the seeds of union within the Third World. It is our obligation to do so. And that is why we must begin by integrating Latin America. Also, that is why the Church has an important part to play, first of all in Latin America and then for the Third World. Our aim would not be for the prestige of Latin America, nor to create new Christian countries, nor to assure a monopoly or even a hegemony. Quite simply our aim would be not to sin by omission; quite simply, to serve."

It was my turn to recall another dream of Dom Helder's, one among so many others. This one is dated January 1963, just after the first session of the Vatican Council. It was "the desire to see the Church participate spiritually in the struggle that will end worldwide injustice. . . . This leads us to think of a Christian Bandung. Let us imagine the moral repercussion that would be felt throughout the world from such a meeting—let us say, held in Jerusalem, halfway between the Orient and the Occident—presided over personally by the pope, a meeting of bishops and Christian technicians from Latin America, Asia, and Africa. It would be less a matter of reaching specific formulas and immediate solutions, and more a matter of taking a stand, of setting the tone, of proving interest in collaboration."[6]

That dream, like others, still remains to be realized.

Meanwhile, Dom Helder keeps on speaking out in public, but his vision has not really taken the form of a program. The question still remains as to what ways and means to advocate a rapid and effective liberation of the Third World from the hold of imperial-isms. By what stars can we guide ourselves in that endeavor? Where are the brains that will give the signal and indicate the direction to take? What are the possible or desirable ideological and political models on which to base reforms that will advance the cause of justice and liberty?

"If the Church in Latin America uses its moral force—and only its moral force—in an effort to promote dialogue between our universities by first creating in each of them groups of thoughtful people in the various disciplines, always with the aim of finding models for our countries, then leaders will at once appear. There would already be a beginning. And afterward, if the Latin American universities dialogue with the universities of Asia, Europe, and North America . . . "

The phrase trails off in a wide gesture of the hand.

Dom Helder does not build programs in the air; he is no armchair strategist. He needs dialogue, needs a sounding-board, needs contact with living matter. For years and years, in the Third World as in the United States or in Europe, research teams carry out analyses of conditions and try to find "models." But it would seem that they have not as yet been kindled by the intuition of the archbishop of Recife, whose judgments leave plenty of room for creative inspiration.

"Personally," he tells me, "I am not convinced that capital-ism or neocapitalism represent anything good for us in Latin America. But the socialist models of today all seem unworkable for us in our situation."

Dom Helder sees capitalism, both old and new style, at suf-ficiently close range to judge its worth, and the model seems no better than its substitutes.

"The United States" he says, "is a living demonstration of the internal contradictions in the capitalist regime. It manages to create underdeveloped strata in the very heart of the richest country in the world. There are 30,000,000 inhabitants of that richest country who are living in conditions unworthy of human beings. The U.S.A. manages to arouse fratricidal conflicts between the whites and blacks; with the pretext of anticommunism, but in fact out of a thirst for prestige and expansion of its sphere of influence, it conducts the most shameful war the world has ever known. The dominant system in the United States is so irrational that it seems to be creating a one-dimensional robot existence which leads the young of various cultural traditions to feel impelled to construct a more just and more humane society, a new social context for humanizing technology."[7]

His judgment on "the supreme embodiment of socialism," Soviet Russia, is no more indulgent, but it is no longer the inhumanity of the regime that takes first place, but rather its ideological sectarianism.

"I do not at all like the Russian 'model,' " Dom Helder tells me. "It seems to me primitive, elementary. Russia still interprets Marxism as a dogma: what was true in Marx's time is still professed in Moscow as *the* truth. Since Marx denounced a religion which, in his time, was the opium of the people, Communists continue to see and to persecute religion as an alienated and alienating force, whereas we have, right here, the living proof of a Christianity which is no longer either alienated or alienating but just the contrary. Soviet Russia, however, cannot concede that a certain pluralism exists within socialism."

"And what about Mao-Tse-tung, Peking, Red China?"

"As for China, it gives me another impression. Obviously it is very difficult to get direct evidence here. But it seems to me that Mao has retained, from Marxism, only the method of analyzing reality. And then, instead of accepting the Marxist philosophy, he stands by traditional Confucianism. Maybe in that respect we can learn something from China. I think we might profit by the Marxist analytical method, which is still viable today. If we leave aside the materialistic concept of life and history bound up with that method in the beginning, we could complete the Marxist analysis with a true vision of Christianity, which presents no obstacle to human advancement, but quite the contrary."

"And what about Tito?"

"For the moment, after the forcible interruption of the Czechoslovak experiment, the Yugoslav experiment seems to me the most worthwhile."

"And Castro? And Cuba?"

"Cuba is too small a country to serve as model for a country such as Brazil. Besides, Cuba has waged its revolution in circumstances that will not be reproduced. The lack of foresight and the egotism of the United States impelled Cuba to throw herself into the arms of Moscow, and Cuba has merely changed one master for another. It also seems to me that Fidel Castro, who is a great fighter, is not a great economist. But even if he must face up to some difficulties, Castroism is irreversible."

On a continent and in a country under a regime where Fidel

Castro was very soon identified with the Antichrist and so denounced, in regard to the Cuban experiment as to the Chinese
revolution, representing the ultimate in inhuman totalitarianism,
Dom Helder has the courage to risk losing face in the very heart of
São Paulo, where he was the guest both of the pontifical university
and the daily newspaper, *A Folha de São Paulo*:

"For how long will Latin America continue to accept the
excommunication imposed upon her sister country, Cuba? Those
who revolted in Cuba merely wanted to see their country
wrenched out of her economic underdevelopment and misery. In
the beginning, appeals were made to Canada and to the United
States. Those who leave a people hard pressed and without escape
from misery are responsible for the excesses to which they are
driven. We are told that to carry on a dialogue with Cuba would be
to expose all Latin America to the terrible danger of 'Cubaniza-
tion.' How long do we have to wait for democracy to be capable
of facing such a dialogue? For how long will we be so naive as to
ignore the fact that by isolating Cuba, by punishing her for the
crime of wanting to exercise the self-determination which in
theory we boast of respecting, is to thrust her more and more into
the orbit of Soviet imperialism and thus create, especially among
young people, the myth of Cuba as a model of revolution and
triumph over economic underdevelopment?"[8]

When Dom Helder's ideas are examined closely it is clear that
he is not, as might be supposed, a man advocating a "third party"
but is seeking equally the condemnation of both capitalism and
socialism.

"I am not trying to find a third way between socialism and
capitalism," he declares. "What we need to find for Latin America
is a line of socialization adapted to Latin American needs."

Some members of the conference he addressed in Paris, in
April 1968, put this question of a "third way" to him and he gave
the same response: "No" to liberalism, "Yes" to socialism, but not
"the socialism practiced in Soviet Russia and Red China." Then
came a programmatic definition of what could be "a line of per-
sonalist socialization."

"I am thinking of a conscious and deliberate participation by
more classes of the population in the control of power and the
sharing of wealth and culture," he said. "I am thinking of a future
when men will become the agents of their social progress; when
the whole of society will attain to a high level of science and
professional aptitude; when humanity will be free, when man will

be the protagonist of a society for which he will constantly be more responsible on every plane—local, regional, national, continental, worldwide; of a society in which the state as subsidiary authority will respect the responsibility of each individual and his entire participation in the life of that society; of a government in which the state will respect minorities and favor without any discrimination a better harmony among ethnic, ideological, and religious groups; of a state where the structures tend toward an ever wider socialization, in which exist and function basic organizations and intermediary and independent institutions that are responsible and organized.

"I believe that mankind can arrive at a rational and functional and planned society and, in international affairs, a self-determination of the nations and a balanced integration."[9]

This reads like a good summary of the classic social doctrine of the Church. On one point, however, Dom Helder is not content with this classic doctrine, at least not with its formulation. Of all the battles he wages, the most circumspect is not the least enduring nor the least important: he wants the term "socialism" to be given respectability in Church parlance. He expressed this openly in the address he made at São Paulo in June 1967. Regarding the two terms of the same problem, he said, "You, the outspoken Communists such as Garaudy and Lombardo-Radice, try to explore the dogmatic monolith of socialism and we Catholics are open to the reality and the concept of a pluralistic socialism." Dom Helder put the idea this way:

"Why should we not encourage the efforts of thoughtful Communists who, disregarding Marxism as a philosophy or theory, rebel against catechisms such as Stalin's, rebel against a dogmatic and monolithic Marxism, and condemn all the atrocities committed against the nations that want to have an aspect of their own, and demand their right to self-determination?

"Why not recognize that there is no such thing as a unique type of socialism? Why not demand, for the Christian, the free use of the word socialism? It is not necessarily linked with materialism, nor does it have to designate a system that destroys the individual or the community. It can designate a regime that is at the service of the community and the individual."[10]

One thing is clear to Dom Helder: "The world trend is toward socialism." He knows, through his contacts with European Marxists, that "Marxism is being shorn of its myths, is abandoning the dogmatic positions that were inherently nonsense, and now tends to liberate socialism from the bond of materialism." He says emphatically, "At this time, we Christians can offer to socialism the mystique of universal brotherhood and total hope, incomparably more vast than the narrow mystique of historical materialism."[11]

That address of Dom Helder, delivered at the inauguration of the Theological Institute of Recife in March 1968, did not go unnoticed. Those who had thought and kept repeating, whether in good or bad faith, that Dom Helder is a Communist, had the proof, now, an outright confession!

Dom Helder had, before this, called for an end to "the false dichotomy of capitalism vs. communism, as if the fact of being in disagreement with capitalist solutions implies an adhesion to communism; as if to criticize the United States were synonymous with approval of Soviet Russia or Red China."[12]

He had wasted his breath, for anticommunism is blind. The anti-Communist is unaware or refuses to recognize that Peking is not Moscow, that Cuba is not China, that Guinea is not Cuba, that Algeria is not Guinea, that Mali is not (was not) Algeria, that Congo-Brazzaville is not Mali, that Tanzania is not Congo-Brazzaville, that Ceylon is not Tanzania, that Waldeck Rochet is not Aldo Moro, that Dubcek is not (was not) Gomulka, that Ceausescu is not Ulbricht, that hundreds of thousands of Communists had hung their hopes on the Czechoslovak experiment. For the normally constituted anti-Communist, all these variants of Marxism are to be put in the same bag and burnt by the Holy Inquisition. So much the worse for the Third World, for Dom Helder, and for some others.

But Dom Helder is not one to abandon his fight for mankind because of dubious arguments over words and ideas. He would certainly be glad if the day came when the pope, when a pope, would take up again and consecrate the word "socialism" in an encyclical: all the forces enamored of justice could much more easily be brought together. Meanwhile there are other things to do than to stand with folded arms and argue.

Especially when you have the responsibility and good fortune to be at the very center of the upheaval that may liberate the Third World: "Latin America is the Christian portion of the underdeveloped world," as Dom Helder has often said. It should therefore give an example of economic development and emancipation, of "respecting the fundamental rights of man." And even to this point: "Brazil has special obligations to Latin America, just as the Northeast has special obligations in regard to Brazil."[13]

One may safely add: and Recife in regard to the Northeast, and Dom Helder in regard to Recife.

At the end of his addresses, his harrangues against the established disorder, his pleas for courageous action in view of rapid and fundamental structural reforms, he is often asked, "And what about you, Dom Helder? What are you doing?"

Dom Helder has told me how he replies to that. He does not talk of his patient work of arousing the consciences of the masses, politicians, businessmen, army men, university students and professors, the Church. He does not talk about the support he gives to trade unionists, students, committed priests. He does not talk about his radio and television programs, or about the innumerable rostrums from which, week after week, he stirs up what his adversaries call "subversion." He merely speaks of a quite small undertaking similar to so many others I had seen in Bogotá, Caracas, Lima, or Santiago, an undertaking not at all commensurate with the great problems of the Third World, but one that is dear to him, as dear as the most miserable creature is to the Creator. He speaks of his Operation Hope.

"Operation Hope is a movement that took its name from a movement launched by the community of Taizé to come to the aid of Latin America. It is a homage paid to Roger Schutz."[14]

Roger Schutz, the prior of the Taizé community, is a personality not at all resembling Dom Helder. He is as much a Swiss as Dom Helder is a Brazilian. But they both have the same sensitiveness, the same faith in God, the same humility, the same patience within the Church, the same passion for humanity. They experienced the Vatican Council side by side, heart to heart. And they have not since parted. A fraternal group of the Taizé community lives and works in Olinda, at the very gates of Recife.

"The goal of our Operation Hope," Dom Helder continues, "is to help the masses become a people. It is trying to arouse minds to a consciousness of conditions. For the moment, the Operation does not extend beyond the diocese, but it has every possibility of spreading.

"The executive secretariat is here, at Manguinhoes, at the Episcopal Palace. It comprises a few experts in sociology and economics, and some social workers. The record of work done so far includes the setting up of fifteen cooperative communities.

"Until recently, Operation Hope had government backing.

After the coup d'etat, there were some big catastrophes here, tragic floods. At that time everyone pitched in and worked together to alleviate suffering—government and individuals. One could not speak of 'councils of inhabitants' or of arousing the masses and others to consciousness of injustices, because it was forbidden; but after the emergency was over, I said, 'Well now! During the catastrophe we were able to do some teamwork. But here, catastrophe is permanent, so let us remain together!'

"Thus, for the moment, the direction of Operation Hope is still partially composed of representatives of public powers (SUDENE, the State of Pernambuco, the town of Recife) and for the other half by private persons: a representative of the council of experts, another of the consultative council, a third from the councils of inhabitants. The organization is too complicated.

"To begin with, we worked rather calmly. For instance, we arrived at a place where the people were living in filth. After we had won their confidence, we asked them how was it possible to bring up children in such filth, in the midst of swine, and we asked them what could be done. We asked them, what do you do with your head and your hands?' And they said, 'You think it's easy? Not only is it difficult, it's impossible.'

"Then we told them, 'Yes, it's impossible if you struggle against conditions alone. But if you struggle in a group, with your comrades here, something can be accomplished. You must try!'

"I assure you, it takes a great effort to set people on their feet and teach them to work together. But it's much more important than to teach them merely to read and write.

"In the beginning, the government was quite satisfied, even when I said to the wretchedly poor, 'It's unreasonable to expect everything from the government. You must begin, you must act, and then the government will come to help you!' But now, after three years of work, the people are beginning to open their eyes and the army is beginning to be anxious about Operation Hope. I'm sure the fourth anniversary of the movement will not be like the preceding one, when we had a whole week of demonstrations and inaugurated three community centers. A community center is really the common dwelling place of people who have taken their destiny into their own hands, they assemble there, and there they continue to work together in preparation for their future."

Recife. It is a town of more than a million inhabitants, where at least 50 per cent of the population live in wretched conditions and where there have been only fifteen community experiments in four years. It is a long arduous task to put one single little corner of the vast Third World on the road of hope. Dom Helder has reason to know this and is aware that all the Operations Hope in the world will still not be enough to rescue all the victims from their present misery. Something better must be thought up, when the fight is not merely for ideas and theories but for the practical betterment of human beings.

"Unfortunately," says Dom Helder, "we discover that even when we make a big effort at arousing the destitute to a consciousness of their condition, it has no effect on a segment of these masses. Some, for lack of health or intelligence, or even because of old age, have no real possibility of improvement."

Dom Helder speaks as if trying to excuse himself. Visibly he is no Sister of Charity.

"I am often told by some people, 'You are running a grave risk in busying yourself with the betterment of the destitute. There's a danger that you will forget to be concerned for the betterment of humanity!' Then I can demonstrate that the major part of my social activity is devoted to the betterment of humanity. But on a battlefield, the wounded are those you attend to first.

"You should see the crowds that fill the garden at Manguinhoes every Tuesday afternoon, waiting to be given medicines. It is our Bank of Providence that tries to help this portion of the masses that cannot wait for true human betterment.

"You know what unemployment is here: the old industries modernize themselves, and sack the workers. When those men are dismissed they do not know how to do anything but the job they had been doing, and it is practically impossible for anyone over thirty-five to find any sort of work. The Bank of Providence tries, even so, to find employment for them. It attempts to train them in some trade or other. It sets up workshops. But while waiting for paying work, they must somehow live.

"I had already, some time ago, created a Bank of Providence in Rio. Today it is a big operation. Every year the Bank has a fair. Every country sends, through its embassies, their best products. For example, France sells perfumes and wine in a red-white-and-blue booth. It's really something to see! And also each province of Brazil sends a product. Last year, in two and a half days the fair brought in 1,400,000 new cruzeiros [$315,280].

"The Bank of Providence can even lend money without interest and without any formality. For instance, when a man is in danger of sinking into dire poverty, listen to what we do. There was, for instance, a man who owned a taxicab, but still had payments to make on it, while at the same time paying for gasoline and supporting his family. Had he fallen into the hands of the regular banks it would have been the end of him. The Bank of Providence managed to lend him a few millions of cruzeiros, in small amounts, without any red tape.[15]

"Here in Recife the Bank of Providence is still quite small. We furnish medicaments, mainly. There are a number of physicians in Brazil. They write prescriptions. But the poor cannot afford to buy medicines. So they come to us and we try to give them what corresponds to their prescriptions."

Again Dom Helder excuses himself. Decidedly, he does not have the vocation of a stretcher-bearer.

"The spectacle of that waiting crowd of indigents gives a very bad impression of unadulterated charity. But I assure you that this charity does not prevent our other teams from working in fifteen different places and achieving wonders in human betterment."

His voice rises and vibrates with enthusiasm as he continues.

"I recall one day when I was beginning this struggle, I was invited by the university students to address a meeting in São Paulo. I was forewarned that some Communists would be there with placards such as 'Dom Helder, the Champion of Paternalism!' Those who had invited me had managed to eliminate the placards, but upon my arrival I spoke out in reference to them.

" 'You know,' I said, 'that I sometimes have a hunch about what lies ahead of me. I had a hunch that there is a group of people here who intended to welcome me with placards accusing me of paternalism! Well now, my friends! I accept the challenge. And I will try to show you that if I am a champion of paternalism it is because I am battling for the improvement of the human condition and for justice!'

"And I told them all about our effort to arouse the masses to a realization of their condition, and about all we had suffered from the government. Then I went on: 'Let us be realistic!' And I began by showing that an entire portion of the masses have no real possibility of true human betterment:

" 'I know what you might say: that it is preferable to leave that portion to rot, so that revolution can ferment. Well, that is your opinion. As for me, I think otherwise, although I understand your anxiety. You are afraid that if I concern myself just a little in caring for those war-wounded, I will forget the war. And I tell you that decidedly I shall not! Eighty per cent of the time I devote to social work is devoted to human betterment. Read my lectures, come and see my work!'

"Today, people no longer fear that I am neglecting the struggle for human betterment. Because Operation Hope is beginning to create problems, and that is a good sign."

On this touchy question of charity and justice, Dom Helder has a story to tell.

"Recently, when I was in Canada, I was asked to address a meeting of a very important trade union. The workman who presided asked me very kindly what a Canadian laborer could do to help the underemployed of the Third World.

"I replied by telling him about a Belgian workman who disembarked at Rio de Janeiro and came to me, hoping I could give him advice. 'I fought hard in my own country for the working class. But now unfortunately Belgian workmen are becoming white-collar employees with bourgeois notions. Well, since I am by nature a fighter, I'm looking for a country where there is still something to do for the working class.'

"I said to the Canadian trade unionists: 'I wonder if it's like that here in Canada, whether there's also a danger here as in Belgium that the working class are becoming middle class.' They smiled. 'Well,' I said to them, 'I have a suggestion to make in regard to that, and I hope you will take it in good part. What you can do of most value in favor of the underemployed in the Third World, is not to send aid. What you must do is try to integrate a fourth of your own population that exists on the margin of the national life. There are 5,000,000 underemployed right here in Canada.'

"This caused a great variety of reactions.

" 'But, excuse me, my dear friend,' said the presiding officer of the union, when he could make himself heard, 'here we have a good law that protects the workman, and the law is enforced. It's not the same thing as it is in your country.'

"And in my turn I replied, 'Yes, but let me give you an example of the flaw in that law. You are young and strong. Supposing that tomorrow when you get to your place of employment you hear the bad news that you are being sacked because a modern machine has been installed which will eliminate your job. Will you be calm and happy, when you realize that, at the end of the month, you will have the right to go to a government agency to receive your relief check?'

"A Marxist intervened at this point. 'Do you believe,' he said, 'that those 5,000,000 workmen who live on the margin as you put it, of the economic, social, and political life of Canada, really have an interest in being integrated into this unjust society?'

" 'Why, no!' I said. 'Give me credit for some intelligence! If I demand the integration of those 5,000,000 marginals, it is because I emphatically hope they will explode the old structures! Five million people cannot be injected into the general society without bringing about some change! I too want to see the social structures of Canada changed!' "

And may one add, without fear of betraying Dom Helder, that the social structures of all industrialized countries, whether liberal or Marxist, need to be changed: the structures of the United States, Great Britain, France, Germany, the U.S.S.R. Dom Helder repeats it often enough in his lectures. Without a "structural revolution" there can be no betterment of the Third World, no justice in international relations, no peace in either the developed or the underdeveloped worlds.

Less than a fortnight before the "cultural revolution," as they now call it, exploded in Paris, May 1968, Dom Helder addressed a large meeting at the Mutualité there. "To the youth of developed countries, both capitalist and socialist," he said, "I have this advice to give: Think less of going to the Third World to incite violent uprisings, remain at home to help in awakening your affluent countries to the fact that they too need a cultural revolution that will bring into being a new hierarchy of values, a new vision of the world, a global strategy of development, a revolution of mankind."[16]

In Recife, Dom Helder told me confidentially: "When I first read the encyclical on the Development of Peoples, I immediately saw that the Holy Father, after demanding justice between the economically developed and underdeveloped nations, was asking the rich, even so, to give generous aid to the poor. This upset me at first. But later on I understood that it was realistic. The Holy Father knows quite well that justice will not be secured for a long time. And in the meantime, charity cannot take a vacation."

NOTES

1. These statistics from the Prebisch report are dealt with in Dom Helder's address at the School of Economics in Belo Horizonte, December 13, 1966; published in *Revolução dentro da Paz*.

2. Address at the Institute for Research on Brazilian Reality, Brasilia, June 21, 1967, unpublished.

3. "Message de quelques évèques du Tiers-Monde," *Témoignage crétien*, August 31, 1967.

4. See above, Note 1.

5. See above, Note 2.

6. "An Exchange of Ideas with Our Brother Bishops," Rome, January 1963, unpublished.

7. "La violence: option unique?" conference given in Paris, April 25, 1968. *Cf. Informations Catholiques Internationales*, May 15, 1968, and *Le Tiers-Monde trahi*.

8. "Requirements of Universal Solidarity," conference at São Paulo, June 19, 1967. *Cf. Revolução dentro da Paz* and *Le Tiers-Monde trahi*.

9. "Dom Helder s'explique," *Informations Catholiques Internationales*, July 1, 1968. Questions posed to Dom Helder after his address in Paris on April 25 were collected and arranged by ICI for him to answer in writing, and its issue of July 1 provides these answers. —ED.

10. See above, Note 8.

11. "I am the Way," address at the inauguration of the Theological Institute of Recife, March 7, 1968, unpublished.

12. See above, Note 2.

13. "Science and Faith in the Twentieth Century," address at the School of Polytechnics, Campina Grande, December 17, 1966. *Cf. Revolução dentro da Paz*.

14. The Taizé community, an interdemoninational and ecumenical Protestant monastic order founded in 1940 by Roger Schutz near Cluny, France. In 1964, Taizé undertook to supply a million copies of the New Testament to Catholic bishops and Protestant pastors in Latin America. Since 1952, small groups have been sent out on mission to serve the Church in the world among the poor in cities in France, Algeria, England, the United States, and some countries of Latin America. —ED.

15. Naturally, the Bank of Providence in Rio has many other activities. It devotes close to two-thirds of its resources to enterprises for human betterment. The "Community of Emmaus of Brazil," for example, is carrying out a task of rehabilitation and re-education of the "marginals," those who are "unemployable," by training them in trades that will rehabilitate them. Installed in zones particularly sunk in misery, the "Centers of Providence" provide basic education and professional training. The Professional Orientation and Employment Service concerns itself with the unemployed, etc.

16. See above, Note 7.

"I Am a Man of the Church"

There are horses
so concerned with independence
that they would rather go unshod
than to agree to go in irons.

RIO, MARCH 12, 1968

5

Dom Helder is a bishop, and even an archbishop. Why do I find it hard to realize this? I believe the first time I was really conscious of the fact·was when, in April 1968, he addressed a meeting in Paris. On that occasion, I asked him if he considered remaining for some time in France.

"No, I cannot; I must leave on Friday, because on Saturday I have to ordain a priest in Recife."

Later on, I discovered among his notes just what an ordination meant to him. He had written, "One of the most beautiful impressions in a priest's life is the experience of spiritual paternity."

I believe it never crossed my mind to call Dom Helder "archbishop" or "Your Excellency." I have never seen him and cannot imagine him with a crosier in his hand, and I was not surprised when he told me he had none. He borrows the crosier of his auxiliary. I can scarcely picture him wearing the miter and I was not surprised when he told me he had difficulty keeping it on his head. I do not recall ever having seen the pastoral ring on his finger. And although he always wears the cassock, he wears it, since the Vatican Council, without adding even the narrowest episcopal edging. There remains the small wooden pectoral cross attached to a neck-chain. Dom Helder does not go so far as to want to be a bishop *incognito*, but he so little resembles the image of a bishop that we have inherited from the past centuries!

"Who am I?" exclaimed Dom Helder upon his arrival in Recife, in April 1964. "I am a native of the Northeast addressing other natives of the Northeast, with eyes turned to Brazil, to Latin America, and to the world. A human being who regards himself as brother in weakness and sin to all men, of all races and creeds in the world. I am a Christian who addresses himself to Christians but with heart open, ecumenically, to men of every creed and ideology. A bishop of the Catholic Church who comes, in the imitation of Christ, not to be served but to serve.

"Catholics and non-Catholics, believers and nonbelievers, hear my fraternal greeting: 'Praised be our Lord Jesus Christ!'

"The bishop belongs to all. Let no one be scandalized at seeing me mingle with people considered unworthy and sinful. Who is not a sinner? Who can cast the first stone? Our Lord, who was accused of visiting publicans and eating at table with sinners, replied that it is precisely the sick who have need of a physician.

"Let no one be alarmed to see me in the company of men who are supposedly compromising or dangerous, men in power or in the opposition, reformists or antireformists, revolutionaries or antirevolutionaries, men of good faith or bad.

"Let no one try to attach me to a group or to link me with a party so that I would consider their friends to be mine and share their aversions.

"My door and my heart will be open to all, absolutely to all. Christ died for all; I should not exclude anyone from fraternal dialogue.

"It is obvious that, loving everyone, I must have, as Christ had, a special love for the poor. At the last judgment, we shall all be judged according to the way we have treated Christ in those who hunger or thirst, who are degraded, wounded, and oppressed."[1]

From every point of view, Dom Helder gives the impression of being more concerned with the affairs of his region, his country, and the world, than of his diocesan affairs. And yet, in the hierarchy of his official duties, he always places the diocese first. But in this as in other things, he knows how to organize, how to distribute the tasks, how to delegate work to others. Thus he greatly depends on his auxiliary, Dom José Lamartine. He could wish that the Holy See might give him a second auxiliary. The way he describes for me his episcopal "apparatus" is very simple.

"I have a secretary. For ecclesiastical affairs I have a vicar-general, my auxiliary, and six elected episcopal vicars.

"The first episcopal vicar is in charge of the diocesan curia; the second takes care of the overall pastoral plan—we have such a plan in Brazil and it keeps to six main lines (unity, missionary work, catechesis, liturgy, ecumenism, presence of the Church to the world), applied by each region according to its situation. The third vicar coordinates the pastoral zones which, beyond the parish, bring together the basic communities. The fourth vicar attends to the nuns; the fifth occupies himself with the laity, and the sixth with the university students and faculty.

"Then, there is the council of priests, whose members are all elected. The diocese has almost two hundred priests of the two clergies, diocesan and religious. The council of priests includes a representative of the canons of the Olinda chapter, one of the military chaplains, one of the civilian chaplains, and a representative for each of the thirteen pastoral zones.

"On the local plan, the parish priests are grouped by zones. Well, so much for the ecclesiastical organization."

Dom Helder is not inclined to talk much about ecclesiastical matters. He tells me nothing of the mission he had programmed for the first six months of 1969. And his diocese is not among those that most often or most noisily figure in the postconciliar chronicle. When one talks to him about the pope, about the Council, or the Synod, the Curia, CELAM, or the Conference of Brazilian Bishops, of the assembly of the continental bishops at Medellín, one elicits from him only words of praise; everything and everyone concerned are sufficiently good and are reason for hope and faith, if not enthusiasm. Moreover, it is the same thing when one talks to him about the seminaries that are emptying, the priests who are secularizing themselves, the nuns who are becoming impatient, the theologians who are putting everything in question, the laymen who occupy the cathedrals, the tensions, the disputes, the conflicts. In all this he finds merely reasons for hope.

Whenever affairs of the Church are brought up, Dom Helder seems to lose all his rough edges: one does not know how to tackle him. The prophet seems to disappear under the patient placidity of the assured and reassuring pastor. Can he be deaf and blind, indifferent and insensitive, or is he being prudent and attentive to his "career"? Can he be one of those Christians who are observed to be as "progressive" in society as they are conservative in the Church, or vice versa?

*   *   *

It is always by way of parenthesis that some rare ecclesiastical problems of the moment have cropped up in our conversation.

One of these problems exists almost everywhere, but especially in Latin America: the problem of religious "feudalisms" that are all too closely associated with the wealthy classes and, through them, with the established order.

"There are some very grave questions to be answered," Dom Helder wants me to know. "For instance, what to do about the congregations that have big colleges. Some think we should sell those luxurious buildings and install ourselves in small communities in the midst of the poor. Others say that the colleges should be maintained, but that the structure should be more open and that working-class children should be admitted. The awakening of the rich to the realities is involved in this. We have set up numerous experiments. In one of our basic communities there is a remarkable nun, formerly Mother Superior of Sion. She came here from Rio de Janiero. Two other very young nuns have already rejoined her.

"An interesting thing happened in Olinda, where there is a Benedictine monastery. Some poor people of a nearby *favela* began to invade the monks' territory. Well! Instead of becoming annoyed and defending their cloister from this invasion, the monks let those poor people remain and taught them how to build houses on the Benedictine property. It has become one of our Operations Hope."

Another question often argued in Latin America is that of the ministry of the priests. It is well known that there are not enough priests and that the foreign priests who, for many years, have come in constantly greater number to work in South America, are still not sufficiently numerous to inspire vocations. An opinion that is becoming widespread, even being mentioned by the bishops, is the fact that the entire method of recruiting priests and training them according to the needs and resources of the basic Christian communities must be revised. Notably some married laymen of those communities should be ordained to serve their own communities. Some bishops have given themselves heart and soul to this reform. But in the debates that have ensued, Dom Helder has not overtly intervened.

"It's still impossible," he explains to me, "because Rome does not even want to hear of it, and in any case they will not allow of a reply. The problem was raised at Medellín. At the concluding sessions, when the final documents were being prepared, there were some attempts to bring up the question. They had to be given up and the archbishop of Joã Pessoa protested.

There were some very lively discussions. But the supreme authority said no, that it was absolutely unsuitable for a document that would have great publicity to touch upon this subject. The authorities merely permitted some bishops who wished to do so to present the problem to the Holy Father directly, and not in a collective and public document."

Still another problem is that of the diaconate. When the Council discussed this and decided on the reestablishment of the diaconate as a permanent rank in the sacerdotal order, a rank that could be conferred upon married men, all eyes turned toward Latin America, which would naturally hasten to multiply the number of deacons, because of the lack of priests. So it was thought; but Latin America has not been in any great hurry to do so. It is in Germany that the first married deacons have been ordained.

"No, in Recife we do not have deacons, as yet," Dom Helder said, confirming this. "At least, not under the name of deacons. For you can encounter everywhere here, in each parish, laymen who are actively doing the work of deacons. I do not ordain them, first of all because I hope for a simplification of the ordination rite. At present it is too complicated."

And Rome has now, indeed, simplified the ritual of the ordination of deacons. But still there are no deacons in Recife. Dom Helder did not tell me what "secondly" followed his "first of all." I suspect him of also hoping for and expecting, as others do, a clarification of the concept and practice of the ministerial priesthood in the Church.

The final problem, strictly ecclesiastical, that entered into our conversations was that of the seminaries.

"Here in Recife," Dom Helder told me, "we had an immense seminary, built somewhat according to the wishes of the Holy See. The building was being completed when I arrived in 1964, and my idea was to sell it. But the professors and the seminarians thought otherwise. It was only when they were finally settled in that they realized how impossible it would be to live in that enormity of a house. We then examined, in our regional conference of bishops, the possibility of closing the seminary, lodging the pupils in small groups elsewhere, and assembling each day at the Theological Institute.

"We sent the conclusions of our episcopal conference to Rome and we received a letter that gave us to understand that the question was settled as we had recommended it. And so everything was ready to begin that experiment.

"But Cardinal Garrone, prefect of the Congregation for Catholic Education, heard of it and sent me a letter saying he was very concerned, that he felt the experiment would not safeguard the essential of what a great seminary should be, and he uttered a cry of fraternal alarm. I replied immediately, saying, 'Any desire of Rome is a command for me!'

"We were under the impression, I told him, that our projects were approved, but that if he would send me a letter telling me categorically to stop, I would summon the bishops and we would halt the experiment at once.

"Then Cardinal Garrone wrote to me again. 'No, no,' he said in his letter, 'if you have already begun the experiment I do not wish to halt it in any way.'

"After this he sent the rector of the seminary of Verona which trains Italian priests who are destined for Latin America; this rector attended all the deliberations of the regional bishops' conference.

"What must be realized," Dom Helder went on, "is that, within a few years, conditions in Latin America will require other solutions for increasing the number of priests. I believe we will always need priests with long years of formation, but in order to respond to the needs of the communities we shall also have to ordain men from those same basic communities. I will never do so without the approval of Rome. But I will try to find the means to show that there is no other solution."

The minor tone in which Dom Helder speaks of the problems of the Church, as compared with the enthusiasm with which he discusses other matters, in no way expressed either blindness or indifference. On the contrary, one can often detect in it a note of impatience, even of repressed irritation.

I think again of that "enormity" of a regional seminary in Camaragibe, that Babylonian monument in the very heart of the Third World. Cardinal Samoré, vice-president of the Pontifical Commission for Latin America, flew over from Rome for the solemn inauguration, May 2, 1965. It is impossible not to detect the evangelical force with which Dom Helder spoke on that occasion. He was putting to the test a radical reversal of the ecclesiastical viewpoints that he discerned only too clearly in that extravagant expenditure of concrete.

"The regional seminary," he said, "comes into being with the responsibility for enriching the concept of development in all its vast human significance, and of adding to it the new dimension that the supernatural brings to human limitations.

"This institution is destined to form priests for development, in the fullest sense of the term. Here will be studied problems connected with the philosophy and theology of development. For example:

"How far can you apply to the rich nations the statements of the Scriptures and of the Fathers about individuals who are rich?

"Is it possible to speak of the 'right to development' in the real sense of the term?

"What is the precise meaning of the 'right to property,' in Saint Thomas Aquinas, the Fathers, the magisterium?

"How do you mark Christian presence in the elaboration of a global development of civilization?

"In this institution the old theological and philosophical themes will be examined along with the new, against the background of ecumenism and the Vatican Council, and in the light of the Third World's experience. For example:

"Reexamination of the principle of subsidiarity, according to the region to which you apply it.

"Studies of the attempts at a new socialism.

"Clergy and laity in the developed and developing worlds.

"Automation and its human problems."

Whether or not the promoters in Rome of the Camaragibe seminary had this idea of its purpose is far from clear.

"Meanwhile, the seminary is unfinished. It functions but is still under construction. And consider this: the regional seminary will grow and expand its influence as the Northeast lifts itself from the subhuman level of many of its people; materially and spiritually they will both grow, fraternally united. In this building of such imposing aspect, we will hope to remain faithful to the Church, which must serve in poverty."[2]

This episode reminds me of another in which may again be seen how discreetly courageous is Dom Helder, who is never at a loss for ideas when it comes to giving significance to the Church.

Time after time in the final days of the Council, Paul VI proclaimed Mary as Mother of the Church and announced the construction of a new church in Rome, and a jubilee. Those decisions caused a variety of reactions in the conciliar majority and among the non-Catholic observers as well as in a part of the press. Were these the most eloquent signs of a renewal of the Church? Dom Helder expresses these reactions in his own way.

As to the new temple dedicated to Mary, Mother of the Church, he says:

"Surely, Paul VI will seize the opportunity to give us two practical lessons: as to the exact place of Mary in the Church, above the saints and the angels, infinitely below Christ; and as to how to go about building a temple on the threshold of the twenty-first century and at the time of a Church that serves in poverty."

As to the jubilee:

"Paul VI has not yet given the details of his very happy idea. We have every reason to hope that the jubilee will bring full pardon for all those censured by the Holy Office and will provide exceptional facilities to our brothers, the priests who have left. The jubilee announced by the Holy Father reminds us and will continue to remind us that one of the outstanding features of Vatican II is mercy and charity."[3]

Dom Helder is neither indifferent nor insensitive nor "ecclesiastically neutral." A new idea of the Church is fermenting within him. He gave perhaps the strongest and most suggestive expression to it in a document, dated January 1963, which swells with the hope raised by the first session of the Council. It was addressed to every bishop who cared to listen, and in the preamble we find Dom Helder saying "I thirst for dialogue. In God's name, dialogue with me."

Not yet archbishop of Recife, Dom Helder was taking cognizance of the doctrine of episcopal collegiality that was soon to be proclaimed and which would put the Roman Curia in its place, when he declared, "Since the Roman Curia should be to the Holy Father what the diocesan curia is to every bishop," and he envisaged as a preliminary, "practical measures to avoid going from one extreme of centralization to an extreme of decentralization." As for the essential, there should be a consolidation of bishops' conferences, national and regional, and "a Senate that can aid the Vicar of Christ in the government of the Church of Christ." It would be the Episcopal Synod.

The status of minority all too often imposed upon bishops must be put an end to, he went on, adding, "It is an understatement to say that the Holy Father is not at all interested in having novice bishops at the head of the dioceses and directing conferences of novice bishops. Seminarian bishops should not exist. This is not a question of arrogant or proud attitudes. It is a question of assuming the responsibility that God confides to us in conferring upon us, without any merit on our part, the plenitude of the priesthood and admitting us into the college of bishops."

Another obsession of Dom Helder is the need for dialogue between the developed and the underdeveloped worlds, in which the Church has the right and duty to intervene. "We have all too many partial movements of the kind, and there is a beginning of collective consciousness. But we still have much to do if we are not to give a false impression of connivance with the established social order, which is unjust and out of date."

A third obsession is the need for "a revision of catechesis." It should abandon the formalism of the textbooks and should adopt, enliven, and stabilize all the forms of the Church: basic education, Catholic Action, stirring the consciences of the rich, bettering the condition of the poor, establishing more schools.

His fourth obsession is improving the relations of bishops with their clergy. "Let us finish," says Dom Helder, "with the impression of a prince-bishop inhabiting a palace, isolated from his clergy, whom he holds coldly at a distance. Let us finish once for all with everything that can give priests the impression that they are seen and heard only through the iron grille of the diocesan curia, when paying taxes or receiving orders. Let us finish with the impression of an authority that is much more concerned, really, with being feared rather than loved, with being served rather than serving.

"Some pastoral visits give the impression of being a 'promotion' of the bishop, in the publicity sense of the word, as well as an inspection of the priest. And these visits are an added burden of expense for the parish. Ideally, the bishop would come as a visitor but would behave as if his purpose was to encourage and sanctify the priest and the faithful.

"The bishop who seems to recall nothing of the Gospels except the driving out of the money-changers from the temple is to be pitied, if he forgets the many other acts of pure and infinite mercy.

"When a priest is sick in body or soul, he deserves to be treated with the care a father bestows upon a son. When he is old, tired, discouraged, he should find in us a father. When he is in danger of falling, he should find in us more than ever the presence of Jesus Christ. There are some fallen priests who want to return, and if for no reason but the jubilee they should be readmitted to the celebration of Mass, even if they have been so foolish as to have attempted civil marriage. There are some who now prefer to support a family, but who dream of the possibility of leading a sacramental life."

His fifth obsession: the laity. "There are some bishops," he says, "who maintain that they cannot find trustworthy laymen. Shall I be thought unjust if I say that we have the laymen we deserve? How can a bishop who does not spend his time in forming his laymen expect well-trained laymen to fall from the skies?

"There are others who are too demanding of the laymen who offer themselves, eager to collaborate. They are too exigent in regard to blunders, or to attitudes that may be imprudent or spurious. We would have more patience with the lay help if we were to compare the little assistance we give them with our years of study in the seminary. If we, even after ten years of formation, make mistakes, what right have we to criticize those who had scarcely any?

"It is a duty of the hierarchy to urge the layman to open new horizons, assuring him of our positive faith in him, and not merely admonishing him to be prudent. We may still have to admonish, but this is so negative. We must remind ourselves that the audacities of today become the normal attitudes of the future.

"In apocalyptic times, it has been said, we call upon the collaboration of the laity, and in times of calm and steadfastness we forget them. Let us integrate for all time, in theory and in practice, the laity in the schema of the Church."

His sixth obsession is "the search for our lost poverty." I have already quoted Dom Helder on this subject, but I will now cite another passage which expresses his thought still better.

"The ideal for us, in dealing with the rich—without humiliating or hurting them, without a tinge of hatred or exaggeration, and still preferring to address the lowly—would be not to distort or soften the striking counsels Christ gave to us. Thus at the last judgment, we will not be accused of having capitulated to or been too complacent with those who have given us alms. It is related that Saint Francis of Paola, when he was given some gold coins by the King of Naples, who had committed outrages and injustices, miraculously broke in two one of the coins, from which blood flowed. In the alms we receive, can we be sure there is no blood or sweat?"[4]

This pretty well sums up the Church according to Dom Helder. These resolutions date from 1963, when Dom Helder was secretary-general of the episcopate and auxiliary in Rio, still only a titular archbishop. About three years later, after the closing session of the Council—he was by then archbishop of Recife—he was to say appreciably the same thing at a press conference but with noticeably less emphasis. Or, as some would say, noticeably more realistic—except on two points, where the demands and hope of Dom Helder are affirmed.

"Four centuries of being 'anti' in theology, in the West, have had the melancholy effect of almost emptying it of meaning. We need a theology that always nourishes itself on the Bible; a theology that drinks the pure deep waters of patristic writings; that is lucidly faithful to the directives of the living magisterium; that is in close relation with the liturgy, in strict rapport with it; that stands firmly on the earth while keeping in view the voyages in space."[5]

He makes a second point: "Moralism and juridicalism have greatly hurt the Church. They are gravely responsible for the abandonment of the Church by some people, the indifference of still more, and the lack of interest on the part of those who could regard the Church with sympathy but are seized with disgust at our phariseeism."

"In saying this I do not forget the Holy Father's allocution to the commission for the reform of the Code of Canon Law. Divine law is obviously sacred and immutable for us and we will all respect the ancient prescriptions. However—and the Holy Father is the first to realize it—our actual canon law bases itself fundamentally on Roman law, which is the masterpiece the whole world recognizes as such, but which, all the same, is a masterpiece of pagan law!"[6]

The years pass—1963, 1965, 1968. Slowly the conciliar reform has spread through the great body of the Catholic Church. But not to the extent of the constantly more urgent demands of a constantly increasing number of Christians who, in Europe and America, have adopted Dom Helder's program, but who no longer see in Dom Helder their prophet. The laymen and priests who form, in Chile, the "Young Church" movement and who, in August 1968, occupied the cathedral in Santiago, demand nothing of him. Nor do those in Bogotá who try to make their voices heard by the pope. No one is really surprised to see Dom Helder bring his acquièscence to the *Humanae Vitae* encyclical on the restriction of births; the dispute in the Church over this question is developing without him. Why?

Here again, a significant episode can at least point the way to a reply.

Everyone has heard of Camilo Torres, the young priest, sociologist, and Colombian university chaplain, who chose to join the maquis and met death in an ambush. Since that time, the name of Camilo Torres has circulated throughout Latin America and the world. He has become the symbol of heroic and irrevocable choice, and the name itself forces others to choose. All true revolutionaries must be for Camilo Torres; conservatives are obviously against him; those who are neither for nor against or who are both for and against, are looked upon disdainfully as intellectuals or moralists without credit and without a place in history.

At the end of August 1968, a great many Latin American bishops were to assemble in Bogotá for the opening, by Paul VI, of the second general assembly of the South American episcopate. Among them was Dom Helder. Señora Isabel Restrepo Torres invited him to lodge in her house and sleep in the very room of her son Camilo, where his memory is preserved.

Dom Helder replied to this invitation in a letter of July 27:

"I received your amiable letter of July 9 only yesterday. I am now asking you to understand the reasons that lead me to decline your kind invitation. During my stay in Bogotá I want to pass as unnoticed as possible. I will be stopping off there en route to Medellín, and shall stay only for the inauguration of the second meeting of the Latin American hierarchy and for the closing procession of the International Eucharistic Congress. Even at Medellín, I will do my best to avoid attracting any attention to myself. The thing that is important is teamwork, collegial action. I feel sure that Camilo, looking down from heaven, understands, approves, and blesses me. During Mass you will always be in my prayers."

Had this concerned no one but Dom Helder, he would certainly have accepted Señora Restrepo Torres' invitation. But whenever the Church is in any way concerned, Dom Helder effaces himself.

"I will tell you the truth," says Dom Helder. "We bishops were about to have a conference of enormous importance; a very official meeting convened and opened by the Holy Father himself and presided over by three papal legates. It seemed to me important to express in my person not the viewpoint of some progressive or supposedly progressive bishops, but that of the entire Latin American hierarchy. I was quite convinced that this would be of the utmost importance. That is why I tried to explain to that good lady why I could not properly accept her invitation. At the time, the important thing was not for one or two or three bishops to play star parts; they should, instead, do everything possible and impossible to reach a joint declaration of all the bishops."

I believe that we have here an elementary explanation for the discretion always shown by Dom Helder in interecclesiastical proceedings. Prudence guides him; but not the prudence of a man who is managing his career. Rather, it is the prudence of a strategist who knows how to choose the time, the terrain, and the weapons which will best assure the advance not only of the vanguard but of the main army—in this instance, the main body of the Church.

"The important thing," Dom Helder has written, "is collegial action." And when one reviews the past ten years of the Church in Brazil, one is struck by the results of that "collegial action." For a long time Dom Helder has stood out clearly against the gray background of a reputedly mediocre and conformist episcopate. Gradually more and more bishops have taken a stand beside him and made themselves heard. Dom Helder is no longer alone. In the eyes of some beholders he is no longer the most representative of the bishops needed by the world and the Church of the future. Others are now mentioned for this position of leadership: Bishops Padim, Waldir Calheiros, Castro Pinto, Pires, Picão, Noronha, Fragoso, Lorscheider—to name but a few. Dom Helder is now far from being alone in defending liberty and justice. He is no longer the first to promote reforms in the Church.

And it is not merely a constellation of bishops who have joined the erstwhile lonely sun: it is the entire episcopal college that now denounces, in Dom Helder's accents, a social and political order that does not conform to the model defined by John

XXIII in *Pacem in terris*. It was the episcopal college that promulgated, in 1965, an overall pastoral plan in every way remarkable; and again in 1967, these same bishops resolutely pledged themselves in these words: "We feel above all responsible for the promotion of fraternity among all men, consecrated by the communion in Christ. We are in the service of brotherly love in its universal dimension, and not only for the benefit of the Church members, but for all men." And this was addressed to a government that is all too prompt to see "subversion" in any enterprise aimed at reestablishing or promoting justice: "We are opposed to movements that are really subversive—that is to say, movements that seek to disturb the social order, taking advantage of anarchy to impose their group interests. Likewise, the abuse of economic and political power for their own benefit is equally a subversion of the social order."

Dom Helder has succeeded in his gradual but certain awakening of the conscience of the Brazilian episcopate as well as the episcopate of all Latin America. But at what cost? He alone knows. How many times has he renounced placing himself in the limelight and boldly asserting his beliefs, which would have won him the ovations of a portion of the clergy, not to mention the world, and done this so as not to deviate from the lines drawn by the Holy See? Again, he alone knows.

I do not want to give the impression that all the episcopate or all the Church in Brazil is unanimously united behind Dom Helder. That would be quite false. The reality is much more modest. But it is enough to illustrate a concept and practice of episcopal collegiality and ecclesial co-responsability, whose grandeur, for those who believe in the Church, is well worth the servitudes.

The well-known writer, Tristão de Athayde, once compared Dom Helder to his illustrious predecessor at Recife, Dom Vital, whose "two years in prison represented a decisive period in the religious history of Brazil: the passage of the conformist Church to the polemical Church. Dom Helder now represents the passage of the polemical Church to the missionary Church."

Indeed Dom Helder represents a "passage," for he is a bridge-builder, a pontiff, and perhaps it is in seeing him thus that we can better see the bishop in him.

The comparison with Dom Vital intrigued me and the allusion to the two years he had endured in prison.[7] But when I spoke of it to Dom Helder, he drew me off in another direction.

"Yes, Dom Vital was one of my predecessors here in Recife—it was when Brazil still had an emperor. One day when I was still residing in the Episcopal Palace I was visited by six men and immediately realized they were leaders of freemasonry. Well, it was precisely the Brazilian Masons that Dom Vital ran up against and it was because of them that he was sent to prison.

"Well, as I talked fraternally with my six Masons I noticed that Dom Vital was looking down at me from his portrait. And the thought crossed my mind that I was committing a sin of treason by talking kindly with those men. But then I told myself this was not so, for had I lived in Dom Vital's time I would most surely have rebuffed them, as he did. And had he lived after Pope John and after Vatican II, he would be where I was, in the Episcopal Palace, trying to dialogue with the Masons.

"They continue to invite me to address them in the lodges, but up to now I have not accepted because there is still the Roman interdict. I feel that I should wait for the pope to annul this interdict before appearing in a Masonic lodge. Other bishops can do otherwise in other countries. But it seems there is a special interdict for Brazil. People are beginning to say that the problem could be overcome, and when that happens I shall pay a visit to the Masonic lodges."

I have inserted this story here because it is significant of Dom Helder's "ecclesiastical discipline," which seems to me to be something other than "ecclesiastical tactics." Dom Helder respects the laws of the Church. Does he judge them all equally well founded? Certainly not. Then is he perhaps legalist? Still less so. I believe that Dom Helder even respects what he least understands in the ecclesiastical institution, respects what clashes most with his prophetic evangelism. His is the scrupulousness of the violent man who is apt to take rather more than not enough precautions to avoid shattering what he esteems above everything, knowing its fragility.

During the night of March 18-19, 1967, as usual, Dom Helder "keeps watch," "pulls himself together," "finds unity," prays. It is the vigil of Palm Sunday. It is the feast of Saint Joseph. And he writes:

"I pray to Saint Joseph, asking him especially to aid the

Church in the hour when she is confronting the reform of her own structures and when some of the best Christians are reaching a point of despair in regard to the Church as an institution."

A few months later, during the night of November 22-23, 1967, on the vigil of "Thanksgiving Day," Dom Helder writes:

"I am grateful for understanding the mission you have entrusted to us. Decisive years are near and will be suddenly upon us in 1968. Thanks for having kept me from the double temptation that has been warded off: the temptation to abandon the institutional Church and to renounce nonviolence."

Three days or rather three nights later, during the vigil of the Twenty-fourth Sunday after Pentecost, he writes:

"Humanly speaking, there will be every reason to succumb. Everywhere I look, in Recife, in the Northeast, in all Brazil, and in Latin America, and also in the world, as far as it comes to my notice, I see the double temptation: the temptation to abandon the institutional Church as a condition for maintaining fidelity to Christ; and the temptation to pass over to violent action as an evangelical necessity in the present situation of Latin America and the world. However, I am still resolved to try other means."

These solitary meditations and resolutions found their public expression one day at Strasbourg. It was April 23, 1968; he had seen the pope a few days earlier.

"The first temptation," said Dom Helder, "is to abandon the institutional Church in order to remain faithful to Christ. However, I will say this: the countersign is to remain in the Church. Not to remain with arms folded or with a feeling of bitterness, but to remain, still engaged in action, coordinated action."

Recalling one day what Dom Helder had said to me of the humiliations God normally allots to every man for his sanctification, I asked him if he remembered others besides the one he had mentioned before.

"Yes, I recall others," he said. "But sometimes I feel that the greatest humiliations should remain a secret of the Lord. But, if my accounts are accurate, there are one or two humiliations that I shall still have to endure. And I mean first-class humiliations!

"The one that would be the most serious for me would be to lose the confidence of the Holy Father. Not only of Paul VI but of any pope. Strangely enough, you see, I am a man of the Church.

"Today, in Latin America and more or less throughout the world, especially among the young people, there is the temptation—one of the gravest—to say, 'Now, to remain faithful to Christ, one must tear oneself away from the institutional Church.' For me, it is just the contrary. I always feel the need to be convinced in my own mind that I am in line with the pope.

"I'm well aware that the institutional Church, although divinely founded, is handed over to us mortals and that we all have our frailties. That is why some aspects of the Church are decrepit. For example, as concerns the parishes, we feel today that the parish should be above all a basic community center; and that where this kind of community center cannot be created, the parish has been outdistanced. The same goes for other institutions. As for the needed reform of the Roman Curia, Paul VI, I am sure, has a plan and it is being furthered, yes, furthered. He cannot do everything at once, but we know he has a plan and is following it."

Dom Helder, one day in the course of an allocution, said this:

"We cannot but be aware that on our continent there are a growing number of people who are ceasing to believe in democracy and are ready to resort to violence, judging precisely that democracy is vacillating and timid, without courage to go to the roots of our ills, is dying of fear, is filled with exaggerated prudence, and is becoming inoperative and useless."[8]

Had he never thought of applying these observations to the Church in order to explain the temptation and the violent impatience he had described? Had he never thought, I asked, that "moral pressure for liberation" might have its place in the institutional Church as well as in politics?

My question did not surprise him. And once more he was all animation.

"Without having the name, right here and within the Church, such a moral pressure has already begun!" he exclaimed. "One day I ran into three or four religious of a fairly worldwide congregation, at least one of the best known, and they were expressing overwhelming indignation. They were thinking of leaving the congregation, and perhaps of abandoning everything.

" 'I assure you,' I told them, 'that if, in your community you feel swamped by others who will not budge, who do not comprehend Vatican II or the needs of a certain renewal, I know of other houses of your congregation in this country. And there is not one of them that does not have a small kernel or nucleus such as yours!'

"And I proposed to them the idea of Abrahamic minorities. No matter what the human organism, whether a parliament, a trade union, an episcopal college, it has a tendency to see its members distribute themselves more or less as firstly, the moderates, who dislike making any great effort, not by nature heroic; this is the majority group. Then, there will be a minority just below that moderate category. And then, fortunately there is another minority above the moderates.

"I believe we must manage to bring about a union of those Abrahamic minorities within the institutional Church. Such an alliance could, like Father Abraham, hope against all hope.

"In Latin America and everywhere in the world there are signs of change, sometimes clandestine movements. Occasionally they ask me to speak to them. There are exaggerations, of course, but this is understandable. There are some who go very far, too far. But by merely listening to them we can be of help. That is what gives me the moral force to influence them gradually to correct their exaggerations.

" 'Yes,' I said to those discontented religious, 'I understand your position quite well! And the ones responsible are those who refuse to budge, who sabotage the work. But since we are here among friends, I ask you, tell me frankly, don't you think there's some exaggeration in what you say? Couldn't you yield on a few points?'

"Well, they agreed to do so. Because within all of us there is a censor, and because everyone, in the heat of excitement, is apt to go too far.

"I believe that if we bishops agree to dialogue with our opponents and not be shocked at their occasional exaggerations when we hear them speak—yes, we must listen to them. We need to listen, no matter what their extreme views. I can say, out of my personal experience, that when a bishop really listens he wins the moral force to make even the most radical person recognize his exaggerations."

I could not help but think, as I heard Dom Helder make this plea, of the all too many Christians who feel shaken to the very depths at the idea of engaging in dialogue with "open-minded" bishops, and, having lost any confidence in the usefulness of such dialogue, retreat and "marginalize" themselves. But Dom Helder has his reasons to hope in the efficacity of dialogue.

"If we bishops," he says, "will have the courage to agree to a dialogue and, instead of taking measures in opposition to our opponents, listen to them, we still have time to carry out reforms. Because there also exist a number of the younger generation who are really moved by the new aspect of the Church. Listening to them I often hear them say, 'Yes, now I begin to understand the Church. I was drifting away, but now I am coming back!' Very often. Obviously what they see in the Church is sometimes her new social and political attitude more than anything else. But that, after all, is a beginning, it is a certain sympathy won. If we men of the Church accomplish this and more, if we can reveal the image of Christ to the point of revealing his divinity, then I believe we can hope for much.

"I do not wish to minimize the difficulties. But I can't think of a single episcopate in the heart of which an Abrahamic minority does not exist. And I continue to believe that if we could establish a true dialogue between those Abrahamic minorities within the hierarchies that exist everywhere in the world . . . One day a bishop of France came here with exactly the same idea, which he expressed in other words. But in France, it is always easy."

"Vatican Council II reminds us that in our quality as authentic masters of Christ's doctrine and, having received the authentic charism of the truth, we are servants of the Word of God and as such it is our task to preserve tradition; to teach is our main duty since we are witnesses of divine and Catholic truth."[9]

The portrait of Dom Helder, bishop, would be incomplete if one did not speak of Dom Helder, "the doctor." The doctoral Dom Helder is as discreet as possible; there is nothing less doctoral than his way of speaking. However, he exists, and once again in a very personal way.

"The hour has come to purify the religion of the humble," was his pronouncement in 1966.[10]

In the Northeast as everywhere in Brazil, and in all Latin America, there is much to do. The people are deeply, viscerally religious; but their religion is very much mingled with superstitions, pagan mythologies inherited from Africa, from Indian civilizations, and elsewhere. It is no doubt a Christian religion, but it often derives more from the Old Testament than from the New.

"What is needed," says Dom Helder, "is to proclaim the true God, by word and example." And he amplifies his thought. The true God to be proclaimed is "Not the ingenuous, magical, vengeful God of our poor people's belief, but the creator and father who, instead of mistrusting mankind . . . and intervening personally to create each creature, elephant and ant, stars and earthworms, has brought into being creative evolution and has granted to man, whom he created in his own image, an almost unlimited right to participate in his creative power. Not the God of the superstitious masses living in subhuman conditions, but the one true God who, having created all mankind in his own image and likeness, does not admit cactus-men or ghost-men to the society of true men."[11]

Dom Helder's governing idea is of "a new Christian humanism," a wide-open humanism that would bring together in one and the same divine plan both mind and matter, body and soul. He has often explained this. And perhaps the best expression of this idea is to be found in the "remarks" he made at a symposium at Cornell University, February 7, 1967.

> What seems to be new and most revolutionary in the religious vision of Christian humanism of our day is the discovery of the full value to be given to biblical passages where man emerges not only as created in the image and likeness of God, but also with the vocation of co-creator and with the assignment of mastering nature and completing creation.
>
> There is no question of forgetting the divine dimensions which bring strength to man as his supreme enrichment. The first step is to acknowledge in man the right and the duty to intervene in history as is needed; of mastering, completing, and leading creative evolution. The Christian humanist, far from imagining a jealous God confronting the scientific and technological advance of man, pictures a Father happy at the progress of his child. We should not fear atomic fission or space-travel or any of the discoveries of the future, no matter how daring and revolutionary they may be. By whose authority can we say that the Lord of life retains for himself all rights over life? That would be a monopoly unworthy of the grandeur and generosity of the Father. And when man grows dizzy with his own power and, forgetful of his incurable frailty, reveres himself as God, the Christian humanist reminds him that this thirst for being like God is legitimate, since, thanks to the Son of God who made himself man, man is given access to divine nature.
>
> An important feature of the new vision of Christian humanism is its understanding attitude toward atheistic humanism. Far from being startled or irritated at the sight of some of the most important philosophical systems of our time treading the path to an atheistic humanism, it rejoices that, although there is a theoretical estrangement from God

to be deplored, there is at least the desire to safeguard man, which means safeguarding half of the law. And he who clings tightly to the creature also clings, no matter how unintentionally or unwillingly, to the Creator and Father.

When the Christian humanist takes a closer look at any of these atheistic humanisms, he finds, without much effort, profoundly positive and Christian features:

Marxist humanism (whose rebuttal of God is based on the mistaken view of religion taken by Marx, as an alienated and alienating Christianity, whereas it is of the essence of Christianity to become incarnate without loss of transcendence, as Christ made himself man and dwelt among us), Marxist humanism, in the realm of economics, gives priority to labor and therefore to man, and so has a central basis for a humanistic economy.

Existentialist humanism has the great merit of keeping us from excessive rationalization and reminding us of the Christian principle of respect for reality.

Psychoanalytical humanism reminds us very realistically (and sometimes by exaggeration, extrapolation, and radical expression) of some dimensions of man that have been forgotten for thousands of years and are of decisive importance to human behavior.

Evolutionist humanism makes possible a new vision of creation, much more in keeping with the greatness of God than a colorless and petty intervention in the direct and personal creation of each being, from stars to worms; the role it assigns to man in creative evolution can be perfectly adjusted to the Christian vision of man and his role in the universe.

"What is lacking in Christian humanism is a better systemization and validation of its principles, and a program of action. It lacks preparedness to meet the great challenge that may devour it: the human promotion of the two-thirds of mankind who today live in subhuman conditions; the humanization of the remaining third of humanity, who live comfortably with this unjust situation and who, departing from justice, condemn themselves inevitably to war.[12]

This concern of Dom Helder for "welcoming what truth there is in all the humanisms, including the atheistic, unilateral and excessive as they have become"[13] is quite as strong in Dom Helder as is his faith in the transcendent dimension which is indispensable to every humanism that tries to correspond to the reality and the plenary vocation of man. This, too, he has said over and over again:

"It is a thing that has been proved: humanism without God

becomes inhuman, antihuman. It is not a question of seeking an issue for our ignorance or an excuse for our egotisms. We have only to recognize a fact: although other demands be strong—the demand of economics which impels us to procure if possible the most with the least effort, the esthetic and scientific and political and social demands—there is the religious demand which gives man a thirst that only an Absolute can slake."[14]

NOTES

1. Address delivered April 12, 1964, upon taking possession of the archdiocese of Olinda and Recife. *Cf. Revolução dentro da Paz* and *Le Tiers-Monde trahi.*

2. Address at the inauguration of the regional seminary at Camaragibe, May 2, 1965. *Cf. Revolução dentro da Paz* and *Le Tiers-Monde trahi.*

3. "A Postconciliar Period Worthy of Vatican II," press conference in Rome, December 1, 1965.

4. "An Exchange of Ideas with Our Brother Bishops," Rome, January 1963, unpublished.

5. See above, Note 3.

6. *Ibid.*

7. Vital Maria Gonçalves de Oliveiro, a Capuchin friar who, at the age of 28 became bishop of Olinda, May 24, 1872. An ultramontanist, he was protagonist in opposition to Masonry and, attempting to enforce a papal decree, offended against a constitutional law. Along with one other bishop, he was arrested on November 7, 1873, convicted, and imprisoned, but gained the emperor's amnesty in September 1875. —ED.

8. Concluding address for a course organized by ECLA at Forteleza, August 1967, unpublished.

9. "I Am the Way," address at the inauguration of the Theological Institute of Recife, March 7, 1968, unpublished.

10. "Science and Faith in the Twentieth Century," address at the School of Polytechnics, Campina Grande, December 17, 1966. *Cf. Revolução dentro da Paz.*

11. *Ibid.*

12. "Religious and Secular Humanism Today," address at opening session of the Church-University Consultation on International Education and Development, February 7, 1967, Cornell University, unpublished.

13. *Ibid.*

14. "Development and Humanism," address at the School of Economics, Belo Horizonte, December 13, 1966. *Cf. Revolução dentro da Paz.*

God Does Not Like Pride

The aviator asked me
if I would like
to kiss the clouds
(the plane would wait for me
a few minutes).

I did not say anything,
not wanting to offend the clouds
but I have never wanted
to kiss the void,
the nothingness.

RIO, MARCH 7, 1959

6

On a set of shelves in Dom Helder's study, as I have already remarked, is an artless little statuette in clay or perhaps colored plaster. It is a likeness of Padre Cicero. I had heard about that miracle-worker who attracted crowds from the Northeast and elsewhere. Why not get Dom Helder to talk about that country priest whose expression was both solemn and jovial? Would it not bring me closer to Dom Helder's spirit?

"Oh yes, Padre Cicero!" he exclaimed when I brought up the subject. "He was a Catholic priest who used to live in my part of the country, in Ceará. I went to see him when I was a seminarian. He was already quite old by that time. He had lost the right to practice his ministry because he had supported the claims of one of his supposedly miraculously healed collaborators, a woman who said that when she received Holy Communion she had blood in her mouth. A commission of experts named by the bishop had concluded that it was not a genuine miracle. But Padre Cicero supported the woman's claims and the bishop suspended him. But he still kept the privilege of receiving Holy Communion, and at his death was in good standing in the Church.

"The remarkable thing is how well that man understood the crowd, how in tune he was with the masses. I recall what occurred when I went to see him.

" 'Stay here,' he said, 'I am going to receive the people. Thus you will have an idea about what I say and do.'

"A man came in and at once knelt down, so great was his veneration.

" 'My godfather!' he exclaimed. 'I must ask you for your pardon, because I must kill my wife Rosa.'

" 'You must kill Rosa? Tell me why?'

" 'My godfather, you gave me permission to go to Piaui. And

when I came back, my wife has a son who is not my son. I ask for your pardon, because I must kill Rosa.'

" 'Come nearer. Look me in the eyes. How long were you in Piaui?'

" 'Almost two years . . . '

" 'How long did I tell you that you could remain in Piaui?'

" 'Six months.'

" 'Well now! During that time Rosa remained here alone, abandoned, without your care, your material aid. Tell me . . . Come closer! Look me in the eyes. While you were in Piaui, did you remain faithful to Rosa?'

" 'Ugh . . . I'm a man . . . '

" 'One more reason! Real strength is not in dominating others, but in dominating oneself. Give me your knife.'

"The man handed over his knife, sobbing, for it's a terrible thing for a man to have to surrender his knife.

" 'My son, if in returning home you have the strength to understand Rosa and forgive her, to understand that she does not need to be forgiven because forgiveness should be mutual, and you have both sinned, then God will bless you. But if you dare to raise a hand against Rosa! Oh, then God will curse you!'

"Another man came in.

" 'My godfather! I have come to see you because I am an incurable drunkard. And my mother tells me that when I am drunk I am another man but that, if I come to see you, perhaps a benediction from you will save me.'

" 'Let me see your tongue.'

" 'Oh no, my godfather! I cannot!'

"Because, you see, to stick out your tongue here is a grave lack of respect.

" 'Let me see your tongue.'

"Then Padre Cicero seized the man's tongue and made the sign of the cross over it three times, saying, 'In the name of God I tell you to stop drinking! Drink no more! In the name of God I tell you.'

"The people attribute some miracles to Padre Cicero. But here in the Northeast that is easy to do. If a priest truly loves the people and if he isn't greedy for money, the people are very apt to attribute miracles to him. Still today a number of pilgrims visit his grave. And especially to wait for his resurrection!

"A friend gave me that statuette because, in a certain way, Padre Cicero is a model."

Dom Helder turned the figurine in his hand, surveying it partly in amusement, partly with admiring affection. However, I seemed to detect some slight embarrassment and aloofness in his words and attitude. "In a certain way, Padre Cicero is a model." Yes, and in sum it is not Dom Helder's way. It might have been. For Dom Helder loves the crowds, the people, the simple people. He believes in the saving grace of faith and in the word that converts. But it is not his way.

And yet, I recall certain things in the narrative of his life as he confided it to me, which indicate that at certain moments of privileged grace, Dom Helder has had what might be called revelations: on the feastday of Saint Martha, during his first "great humiliation" in the seminary, for instance. Did he not say that ever since then the week following that feastday has always been for him a period of grace? Or, again, on the feastday of Saint Thomas the Apostle, when in Rome, his guardian angel "Joseph" had enabled him to talk with Monsignor Montini and to be heard by him. Is there any need to go on?

"I don't want those allusions to be interpreted as if something preternatural had happened to me," he says, "things such as visions. No, nothing of the sort!

"I merely have the impression that God knows the importance of humility for man. He knows our weaknesses, our pride, and as I put it, he purposely sets on our path each day four or five humiliations and, in the course of our life, four or five great humiliations. If we do not comprehend them, if we do not accept them, it's a serious matter. But if we accept them, then we learn the generosity of God. For the small offerings we manage to give, we always receive, during the rest of our life, grace after grace after grace. Perhaps they are coincidences, but they mean much to me."

While I was being indiscreet I felt like risking a little more indiscretion. I wanted to hear Dom Helder's remarks on a certain scandal that had involved a number of Northeast bishops. A financier had approached them, offering them 10 per cent interest on investments in a certain enterprise he was heading. The bishops had lost everything, capital and interest, when that shady financier went into bankruptcy. The scandal was great, for those bishops were known throughout the world for their social commitment. And that they should have lent their money at a usurer's rate was horrifying. Dom Helder had not been implicated in the affair, but some of his adversaries had tried to compromise him. On January 26, 1968, he took up the defense of his colleagues against the calumnies that had been circulated about them. Now I wondered if he had not been greatly humiliated by that affair and I put the question to him.

"Personally," he said, "I escaped being involved because there had been a similar affair in Rio, when I was auxiliary bishop there. I had just barely escaped being involved in that. A financier had injured a great number of people, proposing to them miraculous profits from an investment—somewhere between 15 per cent and 20 per cent interest. Yes, a great many people lost enormous sums in that affair, I had seen it happen. So when this second financier approached me here with the same kind of proposition, I guessed there was something fishy about it and was on my guard.

"The thing that must be known is this: a real problem exists, the problem of inflation. Money melts. It's terrible! Investing money can be understood only if you are acquainted with the chronic devaluation of our money that goes on here. Sometimes it amounts to 100 per cent in a year. It did, for instance, in 1964.

"But although I can understand our deluded brothers, who suffered the consequences for their foolishness, I also understand how completely incomprehensible such happenings are to some Europeans and North Americans. The affair has had a bad effect upon us. Since then, the entire Northeast has suffered from the mistrust of our foreign friends. It is as though they regard the bishops of the Northeast as dishonest men. And those who sent us money before are now holding back, full of mistrust.

"The hardest thing is not the lack of money, it is that mistrust. It's humiliating! But it confirms me in a belief I have. Perhaps we bishops of the Northeast, without realizing it, had become too proud of our open-mindedness, our generosity in the work we have undertaken, and our courage."

After a silence, Dom Helder slowly pronounced the moral of the story, the moral I was waiting for.

"What a subtle thing pride is!" he said.

When telling the story of his life, Dom Helder had mentioned in passing that he had experienced the joy of having encountered a good dozen of saints. What saints? I imagined saints like Saint Francis of Assisi, Saint Vincent de Paul, saints, however, that were still unknown. I was mistaken. He who aspires in humility to sainthood will not model himself on someone resembling him but rather on someone who is just the opposite, in whom he will see and hear the summons of God.

"The greatest saint I ever encountered," said Dom Helder, "is one I can identify for you because his name is known to all: Pope John."

I immediately see the incongruity of presenting John XXIII as the opposite of Dom Helder. One must not be hidebound in definitions. Between the bishop of the Third World and the pope of the Council, the pope of *Pacem in terris*, there is more than affinity; there is a thorough complicity. But I believe I can say that this complicity is not to be regarded quite as much in a similarity of nature as in their absolute selflessness and openness to the Holy Spirit. The fiery Northeasterner, Dom Helder Camara, views the world and lives the rules of the Church as did the peasant of Sotto il Monte.

"Pope John," says Helder Camara, "was an instrument of Providence for a renewal or rebirth of the Church. I tried to observe and study him. And I had the great joy of having three long meetings with him. What moved me the most was his readiness to comprehend, his open-mindedness, his vocation for dialogue.

"It seems to me that today it is impossible to want to establish a dictatorial authority. The only authority the present world comprehends is an authority open to dialogue. If the superior does not engage in dialogue, if he really has no vocation for dialogue, he is as good as dead. He will be unable to exert any force. Now, more than ever perhaps, only the meek shall inherit the earth. I don't say that kindliness, benevolence always manages to be successful in everything. But what kindliness does not succeed in obtaining, severity would not obtain, either. Severity and force succeed only in creating hypocrites and cowards, not the sons of God or the brothers of men.

"Pope John had received from God, had won with grace that capacity of human comprehension, that openness, that vocation to serve. He was truly 'servant of the servants of God.'

"I have known other remarkable men. For example, I cherish the memory of a Brazilian Jesuit, Lionel Franca. That man was really of his time. He was of Vatican I. He was preoccupied with Protestantism, modernism, and all of his books were anti-Protestant, antimodernist, anti-everything. But the man himself was something else, and this memory greatly helps me to understand that at the heart of an attitude that seems to me extremely inadequate for our time there can still be some saints. I knew at least one of them. And that helps me to understand that among those who do not accept our views there can be sincerity.

"There are other saints. For example, I recall a man who, in Rio de Janeiro, was the superior of the Sacramentarians. He too would not be turned today in the direction the wind is blowing. He lived his sainthood in line with that of the Curé of Ars. He often mortified himself, very artlessly, so artlessly that the Father on high must surely have smiled. But he was a real saint and I like to recall him because it helps me to see that the grace of God is poured out more or less everywhere. From that point of view, I am fond of a new Anaphora that we have in the Mass. At one moment there is an allusion to those who are dead and 'whose faith, Lord, is known to you alone.' How many are the persons whose faith, virtue, and sincerity we cannot see but which the heavenly Father knows?

"During the Council, Pope John was visited by a group of fifteen bishops from various parts of the world. It was at the beginning of the first session. We were already sure of the orientation of the Council. The decisive vote on the schema on Divine Revelation had just been taken.

" 'Well! Holy Father,' said one of the bishops, speaking for all, 'you are a happy man! God has inspired you to call a Council different from all others. You said at once that this Council was not meant to condemn, because everything that had to be condemned has already been condemned and more than condemned. And now that you have assembled the bishops from every part of the world, you have the joy to note that the great majority desire what you desire!'

"And, filled with the euphoria, the enthusiasm of those first weeks, these fifteen bishops continued to speak through their spokesman:

" 'But, Holy Father,' he said, 'how is it possible that here in Rome a small group of bishops are obstructive—are sabotaging the Council?'

"There's always a very human temptation to judge that those who agree with us are remarkable people and those who disagree are contemptible devils.

"Those fifteen bishops were there perhaps with the idea of asking the good pope, the saintly pope, to crush that minority. And Pope John merely smiled.

" 'All the same,' he said, 'objection is a blessing from God. Because if we were to go on and on without running into any obstacles, we just might go further than we had intended.'

"Now, that was human wisdom. Then he spoke the words of a saint:

" 'Go now," he said, "go to the basilica and each one of you say what in good conscience you think you should say. I will be here to defend your freedom. But listen, listen! Remain in charity if you would remain in God.'

"Oh, I tell you, those words haunt me. During the Council, very often, I fairly danced with rage as I listened to some of the speeches and declarations. The native of Ceará woke up in me. But then in my mind the words of this holy pope echoed: 'Remain in charity if you would remain in God.' How important it is to understand that God is love and that hatred is truly anti-God, the opposite of God. Hatred and everything related to it, such as coldness."

I can well imagine Dom Helder fairly dancing with rage, I can visualize him standing up in his place at the Council and, letting his anger explode, engaging in a stinging dialogue, to the astonishment and shock of an audience nonetheless captivated by the magic of his speech. Was it to avoid succumbing to the temptation natural to him that he did not once take the floor in St. Peter's?

A few days before this conversation I have just reported, Dom Helder had taken the opportunity in one of those innumerable interviews when everyone questions him about everything, to praise a certain deceased caricaturist. And I recalled that in his program of general mobilization for Action, Justice, and Peace, he had not failed to call upon the cartoonists. Did he regret the time when he had crossed pens with a materialistic lady-professor at the Fortaleza Normal School?

"I'm wary of irony," he said when I put this question. "In my youth especially I was tempted to be ironic. I don't accept irony, even a gentle irony, except with oneself. I am fond of mocking myself.

"Yes, I gave a post-mortem eulogy of a caricaturist. A caricaturist is an ironist. That man surely wounded some people. But from what I had seen of him, I had gathered the impression that he used irony in a constructive way, always. He wounded, but always with the intent of shaking up people, arousing them. If one wounds with constructive intention, it is somewhat like surgery. Sometimes the lancet has to be employed. But I do not countenance hurting merely to hurt."

"I do not countenance . . . " That meant that Dom Helder was not without knowing the temptation! He hurriedly left the room where we were talking, went into his study, and came back with a paper in his hand, a mischievous sparkle in his eyes.

"At present there is a certain movement in our country," he explained, "called 'Tradition, Family, Property,' which is spreading everywhere. They are collecting signatures to request the Holy Father to put an end to the subversive and Communist infiltration in the Catholic Church in Brazil! I don't recall ever having said a word against it. I almost did succumb one day to the temptation to reply. It was just at the time of launching Action, Justice, and Peace. I thought we should aid the humble people to distinguish between true and false tradition, true and false family, true and false property. To help the masses to comprehend that some people who talk about the family say stupid things, all about the horrors of communism, which they say advocates free love, and all this without doing anything to create conditions that would permit a great many working-class couples to have any kind of family life. And also in regard to property, it seemed to me one had to make some very serious distinctions."

The paper Dom Helder held was a rough draft of free verse that he now declaimed with the zest and gestures of a cabaret performer.

There, I may say, was Dom Helder served up plain, in October 1968. Having finished the performance he sat down, caught his breath, and again flashed at me a mischievous glance.

"But after I had prepared the text," he went on, "I said to myself, 'No, no! This shows a lack of respect!'

"I am always fighting for pluralism within the Church. We comprehend pluralism quite well outside the Church, so why not accept, within the Church, differences of opinion on the open questions? With Archbishop Sigaud, bishop of Diamantina and the leader of the 'Tradition, Family, Property' faction, I am on friendly terms. One day, as I left a meeting of the bishops, I said:

'Good-day, Bishop Sigaud. I certainly thank you.'

'But, why thank me?'

'I thank you for the propaganda you have done for us!'

"You see," he said to me, "there are forms of polemics that end up by being propaganda for the very ideas they combat. Today, and particularly in certain regions such as Rio de Janeiro, São Paulo, the Northeast, the masses are beginning to wake up—to be really aware of the facts. So when they are told that private property is an absolute and untouchable dogma, the people clearly understand that it is just the contrary.

"No doubt there is a certain danger of scandal for those who, from the outside, observe some bishops defending positions that are often quite different. But I have a strong impression that it would also be scandalous if I myself waged a war against other bishops."

Dom Helder went on, confidentially.

"I have something else to tell you. I am praised, am continually eulogized. There is quite a lot of talk about me. And so, fundamentally I am grateful to God and those persons I encounter in my life who attack me, who tell me what they think are verities, even if they exaggerate, because human frailty is boundless. That's true. And were I to listen only to words of praise, I might end up believing in my worth, my virtue—and that would be the end of me. Because truly, truly God does not accept pride. That's clear.

"I have some very special ways of protecting myself from those eulogies. When I open a newspaper and see my name, I only read the headline. I glance at the article, zigzagging through it rapidly. I don't really read it. Because, if it is against me and I don't read it, I am protecting myself against feeling hatred for the writer. For it is of capital importance not to feel hatred, not even in the least. I am convinced that God is love. And if it is an article in favor of me and I don't read it, I am again protecting myself, for it is very important not to believe too much in one's own worth. God does not like pride.

"That is what I try to do. But I shield myself especially during my vigils.

" 'Brother mine,' I say to myself, 'Ever since my baptism we have lived together. I merely do what has to be done, always, and you remain inside there, so unassuming.'

"And then, because my greatest devotion is for the Transfiguration of the Lord, I always command my brother who is here within me, 'Transfigure yourself! Look through my eyes, listen through my ears, smell through my nose.' And every time I open my door to someone I appeal to that inner self, asking that he be there to greet, listen, talk. And thus, especially when there are weighty problems, I keep a certain inner freedom. For example, at the end of the day, I say, 'My brother! I thank you, you received the visitors with patience. You must surely be fatigued, worn out. And as for me, I feel quite fresh!'

"The praises that are showered on me—I recall the entrance

of Christ into Jerusalem—I think that I am the humble ass that carries him. Yes, those are the trifling ways to see oneself and protect oneself. Yes . . . "

This faculty of disassociation, of dividing himself in two, reminds me of another conversation—the last words of which may serve as the final words of this book. We were talking about ascesis and mortification, in regard to that saintly superior of the Sacramentarians whose mortifications of the flesh no doubt made the Lord God smile.

"I believe," said Dom Helder, "that true mortifications do not have to be undertaken by ourselves: God takes charge of strewing them throughout our lives. The small problems, the slight events in our lives are sometimes very painful. How hard it is, for instance, to encounter incomprehension, mistrust, when one is sincere and knows that one's thought is being misinterpreted. For example, too, old age: it is truly a humiliation. One must accept it with Christian courage and then, as always, it becomes easy. But humanly it is rather difficult.

"I often say that perhaps the best hairshirts are our friend-hairshirts. In the life of everyone, sometimes in one's own household—it can be a sister-in-law or a stepmother or a sister—there are persons who have the melancholy gift of shocking us a little by their mentality, their ideas, sometimes even by their tone of voice. Ideally we do not let that person even imagine that he or she is a hairshirt for us. This is something like the asceticism of the little Saint Thérèse.

"An objection will be made to this: 'Why, that's not being honest! There that person is, thinking she is loved, and in fact she is a friend-hairshirt!' But you know, in each one of us there are two persons, sometimes three or four persons. There is the old man and the new man. The old man is there who is irritated and refuses to accept. But why always be gentle and complaisant with him and not give the new man a chance?"

In listening to Dom Helder, in having him talk for my tape-recorder while writing this book, I am quite conscious that, at times, in my turn I was as a friend a hairshirt to him. But for me as for so many others, it is the new man who greeted me and manifested himself with patience, simplicity, and joy.

I pray that I have been able to render in all its richness and clarity this evidence given to me!

Thank you, Dom Helder.

Dom Helder Reflects on His Life

When I was a youngster
    I wanted to go out running
    among the mountain peaks

And when, between two summits
    a gap appeared,
    why not leap
    across the chasm?

Led by the angel's hand,
    all my life long
    this is what happened,
    this, exactly.

RIO, JULY 13, 1956

EPILOGUE

I was born February 7, 1900, in a primary school of Fortaleza, the capital of Ceará, in Brazil, where my mother was a government teacher. Yes, in a primary school. You see, the government lacked money to build real schools and therefore gave the teacher a special bonus, which permitted her to rent a house large enough to accommodate her family (in the back rooms) and her classes (in the front rooms).

At the time of my birth, my father had no use for religious practices and so, instead of consulting a calendar of the saints for a name to give me, he consulted a dictionary. There he found a word that attracted him: "HELDER, a fortified town in the northern part of the Netherlands." And he decided to give that name to his son! In later years, some Dutch professors at a seminary I attended explained to me that in Holland, when the sky is clear, people exclaim: "Oh, a lovely *helder* sky! Without a cloud!" I like that. It seems to mean "without complications."

Had all my brothers and sisters survived, we would number thirteen. But my mother, who suffered much in her life, lost five of her children within twenty-nine days, in an epidemic of croup. There were no airplanes then, and in Ceará there was no vaccine. When the vaccine finally arrived, those who received it recovered.

Today, I have only one brother left, older than I by one year, a very dear brother who is an officer in the merchant marine, and a sister who did not marry.

I owe a great deal to my parents, it seems to me. My mother was not highly cultivated; she was merely a primary-school teacher. But she had fine human qualities and the early instruction she gave me marked my whole life. She had a great capacity for understanding human beings and their weaknesses. She often said that if there is evil in the world, moral wickedness, bad people, it is because of human weaknesses.

"My son," she repeatedly told me, "every time someone seems to be bad, we will finally discover, if we look closer into their lives, that it is through weakness. That is why Christ on the cross said of those who had harmed him most, who had stripped him of his garments, flogged and wounded him, 'Father, forgive them; they do not know what they are doing.' "

This understanding of human weakness was transmitted by my mother to me.

As to my father, he responded most sensitively to nature and the arts. He was a journalist, as were my eldest brother and my paternal grandfather. He owned and directed a newspaper in Fortaleza and wrote for it until the paper passed into other hands. He continued to write, afterward, especially theater criticism. I too am quite fond of the theater. An uncle of mine who was also my godfather wrote for the theater and I was always on hand for the rehearsals and even for the performances of his plays. Yes, I am very fond of the theater.

The first school I attended was, obviously, the primary school where my mother was the teacher. She was a bit strict with me. "You must give an example to the others," she said. She demanded a great deal of me, and one day she demanded too much. I remember that I wept and when she led me from the classroom into our house I expected to be whipped—for the first time in my life, since neither my father nor mother had ever whipped me. But when we were alone together she said, "My son, forgive me, I demanded too much of you." Yes, she asked her child to forgive her, because she was convinced that she had committed a fault. It is very important to admit that one is mistaken, don't you agree?

Later on, when my mother could not give me the education needed to prepare me for the seminary, I was placed in another school, a private school this time. The principal of that school was a very intelligent woman who did everything possible and impossible to enable me to enter the seminary. When I left that school I could almost have matriculated in philosophy, but for lack of Latin. I still needed to master that and other subjects when I left that private school, and for this further preparation I entered a minor seminary.

At the minor seminary I made some lifelong friends among

my classmates, fine and devoted men. There was one who was first in the class. Eventually we shared prizes. He was stronger in the exact sciences while I was stronger in literature. I won the prize in literature, not only in Portuguese and Brazilian literature but also in French literature. And then we both went to the major seminary, where he had a greater facility in the moral sciences while I was stronger in dogma. He was stronger in physics and chemistry, I was stronger in philosophy. And so it went.

At the major seminary we helped our classmates during study hours. We had persuaded our rector—a Frenchman and a Lazarist,[1] a remarkable man—that instead of studying all alone, isolated, each one for himself, we should all study together. From then on, Luis Braga—this very dear classmate I've been talking about—helped our classmates in the exact sciences while I did what I could to explain philosophy, dogma, and so on to them.

The only higher education I ever had was at the major seminary. But I believe this effort I made to transmit what I knew and understood to my classmates was of great use to me.

At the minor seminary I had worked hard, but I was a normal boy and at recreation time things often went wrong. Instead of allowing us to talk sensibly with each other, the professors were afraid that a hundred or so youngsters would make too much noise, so they forbade us to talk at all in the corridors. I never could understand this, and I talked. This gave me a bad-conduct mark and lost me the right to go home once a month. It also denied me the right to belong to "The Children of Mary," since only those with good-conduct marks had that right.

With the French rector at the major seminary, I had some amazing experiences. For example, I recall the day when he summoned me to his office to give me some good news.

"I am delighted," he said, "to be able to tell you that you are accepted for the tonsure."

"Father," I said, "I have a request to make. If the Church deems me worthy to be a cleric, to enter the road that leads to the priesthood, then I want to be accepted by the Children of Mary sodality. During all the time I spent in the minor seminary, I was not accepted, and I can tell you, an educator, the reasons why: it was for things of no importance, such as talking in the corridors."

1. Members of the Congregation of the Mission (C.M.) are known as Vincentians in the United States, as Lazarists elsewhere; this community was founded by Saint Vincent de Paul in 1625. —ED.

"Why, of course!" he said, very touched. "Of course you shall be received as a Child of Mary!"

"Father," I said, "I am still not satisfied. Almost all of my classmates are as deprived as I am in this respect. I want to be accepted as a Child of Mary, but only if they too are accepted!"

Well, that day every one of us became a Child of Mary! I love our Lady. And I felt it was important to break up the old routine, to a certain extent, and to make our rector aware that in the seminary this was an anomaly, an illogicality: a seminarian could be judged worthy of the tonsure while not being eligible for a confraternity!

This French rector was given many books by French publishers and, knowing how fond I was of reading, he allowed me to look at his books and read them. It was a wonderful privilege, and it explains how, very early, I became fluent in French.

One day he gave me a book with some pages clipped together, explaining that he forbade me to read those pages.

"Excuse me, Father," I said, "but you may keep the book if you don't trust me. To begin with, I am capable of reading this book except for these pages, even if they are not clipped together. And excuse me again, you who are my instructor, but I ask you: is it good psychology to forbid me to read these pages? My imagination will go to greater lengths! It would be preferable—really you must excuse me for I am not here to give you advice—it would be preferable to allow me to read the entire book. Afterwards, I would come to you and you would allow me to discuss it a little, give you my impressions, then you would tell me what the book lacks, what is uncertain."

Decidedly, that man was remarkable, for he immediately handed me the book, allowing me to read it without any restriction. And from then on, I was allowed to read everything and discuss with him what I'd read.

At that time each seminarian had his personal locker but was required to leave a duplicate key with the rector.

Once, as I was about to visit my locker, a classmate gave me a warning.

"Father Rector told me," he said, "that if you miss something from your locker you should go to his room upstairs and get it from him."

I immediately realized that he had taken some of my note-books, some personal papers. I did not go upstairs to retrieve them. A week passed, two weeks passed, and one day the rector came to see me and find out why I had not done so.

"Well!" he exclaimed. "I said you were to look me up."

"Father Rector, excuse me," I said, "but I hadn't the courage; I didn't want to embarrass you. Because I think it must be horrible for you to see me after what you have done, after going to my locker like a thief in the night. I can visualize you there, with a lamp, opening my locker, fumbling inside it. I didn't want you to suffer such an embarrassment."

I told you he was a remarkable man, very sensitive. Instead of flying into a rage, this is what he said:

"Oh, you are right, so right! But, my son, I found some poems in your locker! And that is terrible! If you give rein to your imagination, your priesthood may be compromised!"

"How strange, Father Rector," I said, "for you to say that, as if you yourself were not a poet!"

"What? How do you know I'm a poet?"

"Why, it's obvious! Your sensitivity for nature and for the arts, what is it if not poetry?"

"Yes, yes, but that is exactly why I want to shield you! For I know all too well what imagination costs me."

"Excuse me, Father, but I'm not afraid of imagination. Imagination is like a sister, a sister that can help us immensely. It helps me to see things, to understand creation, to understand God. Do not oblige me to crush my imagination!"

"I have one demand to make: that you will try to abstain from writing another poem until after your ordination."

"Oh, Father, what you demand of me is terrible. I don't write poems for pleasure. To me, writing poems is like living, like talking. In forbidding me to write poems it is as though you were commanding me to remain silent and motionless."

But Father Rector went on insisting, in all sincerity.

"I tell you, I know from my own experience what it costs to have imagination!"

So I promised to obey, and I kept my promise, for I respected that man who allowed me to discuss things with him. Just think: this was before Vatican II! It was unheard-of for a rector to allow a young seminarian to discuss things with him, and it was still more extraordinary for a rector to admit being in the wrong, as he often did. That is why I made the sacrifice he required of me. I told myself, "This man is sincere, he himself is a poet, he speaks out of his personal experience, therefore I submit."

You ask me, am I a poet, and do I write poems? I reply that my "poems" are not really poems, but are meditations, brief thoughts that I set down during my nightly vigils. In the beginning, I did not tear them up but kept them. Some friends have collected these pieces in small volumes, each containing a hundred or so poems. There are now perhaps some thirty volumes. But one day I said to myself, "I must stop this." I continue writing my meditations, but now I prefer to destroy them.

I can prove to you that they are not really poems, but rather meditations. For example, take this one:

DIDST THINK I WAS UNAWARE?

When everything and everybody seemed remote,
When my fatigue was overwhelming,
When difficulties loomed up everywhere,
A puff of air came through the open window,
Sent by thee, and gently stroked my face.

Or take this one:

LESSON IN WISDOM

The small daughter of the great Company Director
has filled with scribbles
all the books of records
in which important men had studied
the investments that would have earned him millions,
depriving the acquisitive Director
of what peace remained to him.

Yes, such things.

But I must tell you another story about my major seminary.

I feel—it is my personal conviction—that humility is truly an essential virtue. Without true humility, we cannot advance a single step in the spiritual life. But our heavenly Father is acquainted with our weakness. He knows that we have pride and self-respect. I am under the impression that God himself, our heavenly Father, purposely sets in our path each day some four or five small humili-

ations, and four or five big, first-class humiliations during our lifetime. I still remember the first great humiliation in my life.

As I said, this happened when I was a seminarian. One day I
heard that a lady professor of psychology at the Normal School in
Fortaleza was teaching erroneous ideas: materialism, behaviorism.
Today I know that she did not realize what she was doing, poor
benighted creature! She did not understand.

Well, this is what I did. I had been shown some of the notes
taken by this professor's students and I showed them to our
rector.

"We must reply to this!" I said. "We must help the students!
We must make it known that a professor at the Normal School is
teaching materialistic enormities!"

With the approval of my rector and the professors I wrote an
article, under the pen name of Alceu da Silveira. It created a
sensation in the town—a small town where everyone read the
paper. And I was proud! My classmates read the article! I was just
beginning my studies in philosophy, had not yet received the
tonsure.

The professor I had denounced replied and I replied in my
turn—two, three, four, five times! This was polemics! I was convinced that the whole town was excited over the affair.

My archbishop was not there. But his vicar-general lived at
the seminary, and he was one of those saints that God has ordained I should meet from time to time in my life. He sent for me,
and I was absolutely sure it was to congratulate me on my
writings. But here is what happened:

"Is it true that those articles really come from your pen?" he
asked.

"Yes, Father, it is true," I answered, very touched, very
satisfied.

"Then, my son, I must tell you that the article published in
yesterday's paper is the last article you will write."

"Oh, Father! That's impossible! Excuse me, but have you
read the enormities that woman wrote in today's paper? No,
Father! At least let me reply to that last article of hers. I have
already written it and can show it to you."

"The article that appeared yesterday is your last."

I went out, my mind in a whirl of stormy thoughts. For the
devil is rather smart, and the devil was prompting me. "The vicar-
general is a saint," he whispered, "but even a saint is influenced by

the bonds of family and friendship!" For now I must tell you, this professor at the Normal School was the sister-in-law of the vicar-general. You can imagine his temptation! I was eighteen years old, and the storm I was swept up into was terrible.

Fortunately I passed the chapel, and entered it, since I had complete freedom at the seminary, with the protection of the rector, the professors, and my friendly classmates. As I found myself face to face with an image of the Blessed Virgin, I recall that I said to myself, "I shall leave here only when I have recovered my calm."

I am convinced that had I not managed to submit to the humiliation which had been sent me that day, not by the devil, but by the heavenly Father, I would very probably, no, surely, have abandoned the seminary and perhaps the Faith as well.

I remained in the chapel one hour, two hours, two and a half hours. My comrades went out in great silence, going afterward to the refectory. They had heard the news, because the rector had been informed. And with the backing of the rector and some of the professors, they were planning a demonstration against the vicar-general.

But meanwhile I was in the chapel repeating, "Holy Mother, I will not leave this place until I have recovered my calm."

At the end of two and a half hours, I suddenly recalled that it was the feastday of Saint Martha: July 29. And I recalled the words, "Martha, Martha, you worry and fret about so many things, and yet few are needed, indeed only one. It is Mary who has chosen the better part." And I immediately understood that what had seemed to me the defence of truth and faith had been pride. I was preparing for the tonsure in a state of pride!

This cured me. I made an act of contrition. But the devil was lying in wait for me: my colleagues made a big demonstration on my behalf. "Continue!" they urged me. "You must continue!"

But I told them the whole story and recounted the revelation that had come to me.

"Please," I implored them, "help me to understand that it was pride."

The moral of the fable is this: When you give something quite small to the heavenly Father, he responds with marvelous recompenses. Ever since that day, the most precious divine favors of my life are always bestowed upon me either on the feastday of Saint Martha or in the week following.

I was ordained August 15, 1931, at the age of twenty-two and a half. My vicar-general, the one who figured in the story I have just related, made me remain at Fortaleza. He felt that the two who were first in the class should remain in the capital. But my colleague, who was first in the class, immediately refused, preferring to go into the interior. From that time until now, he has remained in a provincial parish, and after all these years we are still good friends.

Meanwhile, in Fortaleza, I had another very strong temptation: fascism. It was the era of Mussolini in Italy, of Salazar in Portugal, and people were already beginning to talk, more or less, about Hitler in Germany.

My archbishop had entrusted to me the ministry to workers and intellectuals. He also assigned to me a chapel where I was to organize a parish.

During that early period of fascism there was a certain Catholic leader in Rio de Janeiro, Jackson de Figueiredo, a strong and courageous man whose political ideas were right wing. He had founded and directed a review called *A Ordem*—Order—until his tragic death by drowning, in 1928. His successor was a newly converted Catholic, one of the most remarkable men in Brazil, with whom I have remained a fraternal friend: Alceu Amoroso Lima. I often say of him, "He would be considered great, even in France."

I was still a seminarian when I wrote a boyish letter to Alceu, when Jackson de Figueiredo died, saying in part, "Fortunately, God has called you to replace him. How glad I am to have you as leader! " Alceu immediately answered with a very kind and open-hearted letter, telling me about a young lieutenant, Severino Sombra, who had just arrived in Ceará. "You must go to see him," he wrote, "and try to work with him while you are still at the seminary and especially after your ordination." I continued to write to Alceu, and made the acquaintance of the young lieutenant.

And this young lieutenant in his turn put me in touch with still another lieutenant. I did not know this one personally, but for a whole year we exchanged letters, because he wanted to re-examine Christian doctrine. After his first Communion he had drifted away from the Faith. We each wrote twice a week. In one of his letters he said, "Intellectually, I haven't the least doubt; but I do not have faith." It was the first time that I had experienced the fact that there is truly something over and above the arguments: heavenly grace. After some reflection I told him, "Perhaps it is because of a feeling of pride. Put on your uniform, go to church and kneel down in front of everyone. And try to be humble." But it did no good, faith did not come to him.

One day he came to see me—it was our first meeting. He found me with a book in my hands: Saint Thérèse's autobiography, *The Story of a Soul.*

"Let me see the book," he said.

"No, it's not for you, as yet. Perhaps later on, when you have faith."

But he insisted and borrowed the book. And the next day he wrote me a short note: "What you did not manage to obtain, the little Thérèse obtained in a few minutes."

Why am I talking about those two young lieutenants? It's because we began a movement among intellectuals and workers, which we called the "October Legion"—with brown shirts! Severino Sombra was already very much interested in Salazar and expected much of Portugal, the corporate state, for he believed this was the way to safeguard democracy.

Shortly after this movement began, Plinio Salgado launched "integralism," the Brazilian form of fascism. He wrote to Severino Sombra, inviting him to establish integralism in Ceará, and asked me to be secretary of education for the movement in that state. As usual, I asked my bishop for his advice. I explained the aims of the movement, told him it was still in the process of formation, that what it would end up in was still unclear, and I said I believed that many young workers would join, but that I would do nothing without his advice.

"If you tell me yes, then it's yes," I said. "And if you tell me no, then it's no."

My bishop studied the papers I had brought with me and finally said that I should accept. So that is how I became an Integralist.

At that period I had the idea that the world was about to split in two: the Left and the Right, communism and fascism.

Within the Integralist movement we talked of God, the Fatherland, and the family. We were very sincere. The movement attracted some remarkable young people. Many great men I was later to meet in public life were Fascists at that time.

I remained a part of the movement for nearly two years.

One day my archbishop organized a big electoral action. This was in 1934, and we in Brazil were about to be given a new constitution. The Church was very preoccupied with it, and Cardinal Leme, archbishop of Rio de Janeiro, thought up the idea of organizing an "Electoral League" throughout the country. Properly speaking, it was not a political party. The Church merely presented certain demands to the candidates of the various parties, outlining a constitutional program to which they were asked to commit themselves. What my archbishop demanded of me was to carry out a campaign in favor of the candidates who agreed to the program of the Electoral League in Ceará.

Blindly I obeyed the bishop. I campaigned throughout the state, and all the candidates who had signed, and only those candidates, were elected.

The governor-elect was naturally very pleased with these results, and he succeeded in convincing my bishop that I should be Secretary of Education for the state, while I did everything I could to avoid being officially nominated.

"During the entire campaign," I told my bishop, "I said I was not pleading my own cause. And now you are obliging me to accept!"

"You must, you must, because it is a post of immense importance."

So that is how I was appointed, while quite young, to be Secretary of Education in my home state in Ceará. I went to speak with the governor.

"You know that I belong to the Integralist movement," I told him. "But I haven't the slightest intention of playing politics, not even minipolitics, in my post as Secretary of Education. Nor should you play politics either. I accept the post only on these conditions."

The governor accepted my terms.

Then I entered into correspondence with a Brazilian educator of exactly my own age, twenty-four, who had been called to Rio to work out educational reforms. This man, Lourenço Filho, was a remarkable pedagogue. He gave me the help I needed. But then the governor began to play minipolitics in my sector of education, and I immediately went to tell my archbishop that I could not tolerate this and that I was handing in my resignation. Then I wrote to notify Lourenço Filho. He replied by wire: "If you leave the Secretariat of Education, I invite you to come to Rio de Janeiro as expert advisor to the federal Secretariat."

My archbishop was rather glad to see me leave, for this spared him difficulties with the local government.

And that is how I happened to arrive in Rio in 1936.

At that time I was twenty-seven years old and I was to live in Rio for twenty-eight years—longer than I had lived in my native province.

I was appointed technical assistant at the Ministry of Education of the municipality of Rio de Janeiro, capital of Brazil. Eventually I was summoned to work at the Institute for Educational Research, at the head of a service that was setting up programs and likewise the tests for pupils in the public schools of Rio.

Cardinal Leme entrusted me with the technical direction of religious education for the renewal of catechetical instruction.

At our very first meeting, the cardinal told me how glad he was to have me in Rio. But since he was aware that I had joined the Integralist movement at the request of my archbishop of Fortaleza, he asked me to leave that movement, making the demand in his function as archbishop of Rio.

The Ministry of Education then created the post of "Expert in Education," for which one had to pass a competitive examination, and I asked permission of Cardinal Leme to take the exam. I realized that I had arrived in Rio without having given any proof of my capability and that I was responsible for setting up programs and tests for almost 120,000 pupils in the city's public schools, with eighteen experts in my service.

The cardinal gave me permission; I passed the government test and was appointed Expert in Education.

Shortly afterward I went to see my cardinal.

"You know," I told him, "I feel I am doing work that a layman could do very well, and am failing to perform the tasks of a specifically priestly nature."

He did not agree with me and would not let me leave my post, because he thought I could have an immense influence there and that by my presence alone I could do a great deal of good. But after his death, his successor, Cardinal Jaime de Barros Camara, understood my reasons and I was allowed to hand in my resignation. The government, however, immediately appointed me to membership in the Education Council, and so I remained in Rio until I left for Recife in 1964.

In Rio at that time there was a papal nuncio who afterward became cardinal: Carlo Chiarlo. One day he summoned me to propose another employment of my energies.

"Papal nuncios," he said, "are all too frequently in the hands of local councillors and unfortunately I have not been entirely satisfied with mine. But I have closely studied the question and I feel sure that you would make a good councillor. I want you to come to see me every Saturday in order to help me study Brazilian problems."

So it was that every week I went to the nuncio's residence and was able to help a little in the nomination of bishops. And when I saw the hierarchy continually expanding in this country, which is as vast as a continent and with poor communications, I had an idea that I presented to the nuncio.

"Brazil should have a conference of bishops," I said. "A secretariat must be put at their service. The bishops have no time to read or study. A secretariat, with experts to suggest and consider problems, could help the bishops make decisions."

I returned again and again to this idea. In 1950, taking advantage of the Holy Year in Rome and of the World Convention of Lay Apostles, I went to Rome. It was my second visit. With the help of some priests and laymen, I had prepared eighteen proposals for this convention. All my arguments ended in the same way: none of all this would be possible without the organization of the local hierarchy.

The nuncio had me go to Rome for the lay convention, with my proposals, and he entrusted me with his mail-pouch for the Vatican, which would enable me to speak with Monsignor Montini. He appended a letter saying that I, "Monsignor Camara," had the full confidence of the nunciature and of the Brazilian bishops, and that I had things to say that could be of importance.

I well remember my arrival in Rome! Immediately I took the pouch to the Secretariat of State, leaving with it the text of my eighteen proposals, especially underlining the conclusions. And Monsignor Montini very amiably and clearly told me, "I will call you."

Well, I waited and waited for that call, in a small unheated *pensione*—unheated, and this in December. One morning I woke up to discover that I was deaf and that blood was running out of my ears. I could not hear a thing. When I said Mass I could hear nothing. A Brazilian seminarian who was there spoke to me and I couldn't hear him. I recall that it was the feastday of Saint Thomas the Apostle when this occurred.

Upon my return from Mass I was told that in my absence I had had a telephone call from the Secretariat of State. The message that had been left was that I should report to Monsignor Montini that afternoon at one o'clock. That very day!

Even before this sudden loss of hearing, I had one big problem: I would have to speak in French. If my French is still faulty today, you can imagine what it was like twenty years ago! But I had a personal faith in my guardian angel. I call him Joseph, because I do not yet know his name, and because my mother, when very pleased with her son, called him Joseph. So I prayed to him:

"Joseph, today I must talk with Montini. Now, if this idea of a conference of bishops is my personal invention and if I have any ulterior motives, then let me remain deaf, let me not hear a thing! And let my French not function! But if my idea is really sound, then I ask two favors of you: let me hear Montini and let me manage to transmit my message."

When I arrived at the door of the Vatican—I was a monsignor then, but was wearing no red—they would not let me in.

"Oh, no!" they said, "it's almost Christmas! Impossible."

"But I tell you, Monsignor Montini telephoned me to come here."

They would not believe it. Then I thought that perhaps someone had been fooling me. But it was the feastday of Saint Thomas, so I gathered all my courage together—I am naturally rather timid—and insisted.

"I request you to do this for me," I said, "it would be easy for you to telephone the Secretariat. Be so kind as to do so."

And they telephoned and found it was true that I was expected. Phew! I was soon in the elevator!

After a good half hour of conversation Monsignor Montini was convinced.

"Monsignor," he said to me, "I am won over to the idea of a conference of the Brazilian bishops. We must create it. But I still have one doubt . . . "

That is typically Montini! He remains the diplomat who, at a certain moment, makes a test. He submitted me to one.

"If I understand your idea aright," he said, "it concerns a conference of bishops. From what I've read in these reports, the key man, the man to tie this thing up would be you, Monsignor. But you are not a bishop. And so?"

"Excuse me, Monsignor," I said. "I am not sure I've understood you. Please put your question more clearly."

He then stated the problem clearly and unmistakably!

"You are not a bishop, yet you would be the key man to tie this thing up." And he asked if I entertained the ambition to become a bishop.

"Excuse me, Monsignor," I said, "I would countenance this doubt if it were expressed by any other person, but not by you. Because I know Your Excellency is highly placed, yet you are not a bishop. Even so, God uses you as the key man to handle the worldwide episcopacy."

Montini smiled at this and our friendship was born! He had discovered that I had no ulterior motive.

"Be assured," he said, "we will examine the documents, and the conference shall be created."

A year afterward the conference had not yet been created. The nuncio found a way to send me back to Rome, and when I was again in the presence of Montini, he recognized me.

"Oh!" he said. "We still owe a debt to Brazil! But I assure you, two months from now, the conference will be created."

And in fact the National Conference of the Bishops of Brazil (CNBB) was created and I was named secretary general, a post I held for twelve years—two periods of six years.

Later on, after the Eucharistic Congress of Rio, since the Brazil conference was going ahead well, the Holy Father created similar conferences in all the Latin American countries. And then there was CELAM, the Latin American bishops' council for the whole continent.

Cardinal Camara was very fond of me, so one day in 1952 he requested that I be named auxiliary bishop, then auxiliary archbishop in 1955, the year when I was entrusted with organizing the International Eucharistic Congress in Rio de Janeiro and the first Latin American bishops' conference.

Thus I have never exercised any parish ministry. But I was

always director of religious instruction. And I preached all the time in the churches of Rio and I preached some retreats and spiritual conferences. I was general chaplain of Catholic Action. I always had my confessional. I followed more particularly a group of remarkable souls, the dearest friends I still have in Rio.

I knew that the cardinal loved me like a son. His only concern was about my involvement in so much noisy activity and so showered with praise. He was afraid that all this commotion around me would do me harm. Yes, he cared for me like a father.

After the International Eucharistic Congress I had a visitor from France: Cardinal Gerlier, of Lyons. He shut the door behind him before telling me the purpose of his visit.

"I have had some experience in organization," he said, "and since taking part in this Eucharistic Congress I must tell you that you have exceptional capacities as an organizer. This is not a compliment I am paying you. I say it instead to awaken you to a sense of responsibility. Now, I ask you: why do you not put those capacities of yours to work at solving the problem of the slums, what you call the *favelas*?"

Thus, Cardinal Gerlier was the one who gave me the push that plunged me into this action. Formerly, I had felt the problem, but had not been involved in the battle.

But my cardinal, who took a fatherly interest in me, wanted me above all to remain humble and simple-hearted. For that reason he was afraid of seeing me involved in this struggle. In my efforts to reassure him, I took him, one day, a book I had written, completely finished although I had no intention of having it published. My subject was the presence of God. I called to mind, for the assistance of the reader, the multiple ways God has of showing his presence.

My cardinal was very pleased and he almost succeeded in persuading me to have the book published. He even wrote a preface. But I have never thought of publishing anything of any kind during my lifetime. After my death my writings can be published, but not before.

One day—it was the feast of Saint Vincent de Paul—the cardinal was saying a very solemn Mass, and afterward I pronounced the eulogy. I seized the opportunity to present to my cardinal a complete survey of what I thought of social problems. I tried to say that the important thing to remember about Saint Vincent is not what he did—for that is well known and needs none of our praise. Instead, we should meditate on the question: What would Saint Vincent de Paul do today? What would be the principal manifestations of his charity? To sum up: Saint Vincent de Paul's charity today would be to do justice.

After this eulogy, Cardinal Camara realized that from then on and in the future we would inevitably draw more and more apart. We are in close agreement when we recite the *Credo*. But in open questions, he feels that communism is the greatest social problem, while I was and still am convinced that the greatest problem is social injustice.

Not long afterward, a few years later, our separation became a fact.

"My son," he said to me one day, "I see that the only way for us to remain good friends is to part. We must do as Saint Paul and Saint Barnabas did. Each of us must do all we are capable of doing, but we must go our separate ways."

"Oh, my cardinal!" I said. "How pleased I am with your straightforwardness. It is the lack of your kind of courage that always depresses me. It always depresses me to see the lack of this sort of honesty among Christians, priests, even bishops. For you to tell me frankly that you are considering separating from me takes remarkable courage. I thank you with all my heart and I give you every right to talk to the Holy Father on the subject. I will raise no objection if I am told to go to any diocese whatsoever."

The nuncio, Archbishop Lombardi, who was like a brother to me and was well aware what it would cost me to leave Rio de Janeiro after twenty-eight years there, was obliged to initiate the procedure.

One day I received a query from Rome asking me if I would accept an appointment as apostolic administrator in Salvador da Bahia. I immediately replied that I had no objection, as the Holy Father must know, since he had absolute power over my life. But there was one difficulty, not for me but for the bishop of Salvador, who would no longer have any power and would merely retain his rank of cardinal. When he had received the letter from Rome he had replied at once, asking that what had been done be cancelled, since such and such a cardinal and such another cardinal older than he remained at the head of such and such a Sacred Roman Congregation, and such another Congregation, with many examples.

I had been on the point of leaving for Rome at that very

time. It was in 1964, during the intercession of the Council, and I belonged to a commission. The nuncio had confided to me his feelings that the Holy Father would not force the issue of my appointment to Salvador. But he was disturbed because the only vacant diocese for me was the small diocese of São Luis do Maranhão, to the north.

"But, my dear nuncio," I said, "let us leave all this in the hands of God."

As it turned out, the Holy Father did not want to insist on sending me to Salvador, where I would have outweighed the cardinal in authority. Nor did he want to appoint me to São Luis do Maranhão.

"Holy Father," I said, "if the cardinal of Rio de Janeiro urges you, and if the only vacant diocese is São Luis do Maranhão, we must see the hand of God in all this! As for me, I accept."

At one o'clock that afternoon, I was therefore named archbishop of São Luis do Maranhão. It was a beautiful Roman day. I was satisfied, because I was quite convinced that it was the will of God. But at four-thirty I received a cable from the nuncio, which would have been meaningless in other circumstances, informing me of the sudden death of the archbishop of Recife.

Next day I was summoned to the presence of the Holy Father. Naturally he had also received the news. He was sad, but he remarked that God knew how to derive good from sorrow and he saw in this a sign of Providence that called me to Recife. And he wanted my nomination to be published the following day, without any other procedure.

"Holy Father," I said, "you have now as always complete freedom to manage my life without even asking my personal advice. But if I may be allowed to say so, I would prefer not to have the nomination announced tomorrow, because it is too close to the archbishop's death."

Thus it was a week, but only a week, after the death of the archbishop that my nomination was announced. That was in March 1964. And on the first of April there was a "revolution" in Brazil. On April 12, I took possession of the diocesan center of Recife.

I seized the occasion to speak out my thoughts very clearly, knowing that if God did not give me courage at that time, at my entrance into the diocese, afterward it would be too late.

And I have tried to say what I thought ever since. ■